Coal

## Resources series

# Coal

Mark C. Thurber

polity

First published in 2019 by Polity Press

Polity Press
65 Bridge Street
Cambridge CB2 1UR, UK

Polity Press
101 Station Landing
Suite 300
Medford, MA 02155, USA

ISBN-13: 978-1-5095-1400-7
ISBN-13: 978-1-5095-1401-4(pb)

A catalogue record for this book is available from the British Library.

Library of Congress Cataloging-in-Publication Data

Names: Thurber, Mark C., author.
Title: Coal / Mark C. Thurber.
Description: Cambridge ; Medford, MA : Polity Press, 2019. | Includes
  bibliographical references and index.
Identifiers: LCCN 2018041738 (print) | LCCN 2018058185 (ebook) | ISBN
  9781509514045 (Epub) | ISBN 9781509514007 (hardback) | ISBN 9781509514014
  (pbk.)
Subjects: LCSH: Coal--Environmental aspects. | Coal mines and
  mining--Environmental aspects. | Energy policy. | Energy security. |
  Environmental policy. | Power resources.
Classification: LCC TD196.C63 (ebook) | LCC TD196.C63 .T44 2019 (print) | DDC
  333.8/22--dc23
LC record available at https://lccn.loc.gov/2018041738

Typeset in 10.5 on 13pt Scala by
Servis Filmsetting Ltd, Stockport, Cheshire
Printed and bound in Great Britain by CPI Group (UK) Ltd, Croydon

For further information on Polity, visit our website: politybooks.com

# Contents

# Figures and Boxes

# Acknowledgments

I am very grateful to the many people who contributed to this book. Frank Wolak was an invaluable sounding board and source of encouragement. Various subject matter experts read early drafts and shared their considerable expertise, notably including Bart Lucarelli, on everything under the sun related to coal; Kevin Jianjun Tu, on coal in China (and everywhere else); Peter Hughes, on the competition between coal and natural gas; and Roger Stern, on mineral scarcity ideology. I learned a great deal from all of my co-authors on my previous coal book project; insights I gained from their work are sprinkled liberally throughout this volume. I owe an important debt to two former colleagues at the Program on Energy and Sustainable Development at Stanford University, David Victor and Richard Morse, who helped inform my thinking about how the challenges around coal will shape the world's energy and environmental future. Kyeyoung Shin provided helpful research assistance on air pollution impacts of coal and public opinion about different energy sources.

I thank the four anonymous reviewers whose comments helped make this book substantially better. One reviewer went above and beyond the call of duty to make detailed suggestions throughout the text, nearly all of which have been incorporated in the final version.

The team at Polity did a terrific job of shepherding this book through the publication process from start to finish.

I am grateful to Louise Knight, for launching the project and working with me to make the manuscript better; to Nekane Tanaka Galdos and Sophie Wright, for keeping me well informed throughout the process; to Evie Deavall, for managing production; and to Susan Beer, for expert copyediting.

My wife Nancy was the first person in our family to study coal, and I am especially grateful for her love and support. I also thank Michelle and Jeremy for their enthusiasm for everything I write.

It goes without saying that any inaccuracies or other shortcomings in the text are mine and mine alone.

# CHAPTER ONE

# The Double-Edged Sword of Coal

## Fueling the world with coal

The modern, industrialized character of life today can be traced directly back to coal. Coal liberated industrial production from dependence on energy from water and trees. It created a self-reinforcing cycle of industrialization. Coal made iron and steel, which made steam engines, which helped mine and transport more coal. A coal-fueled Industrial Revolution started in Britain in the late 1700s and spread to the rest of Europe, to North America, and beyond.

Since then, the scale of global coal use has only grown. In 2015, coal was used to produce approximately 28% of the total primary energy consumed worldwide.[1] Coal's most significant role is in generating electricity, an application in which it is the leading energy source, with a 39% share (see Figure 1.1). But coal is also burned to produce heat for industrial processes, and in some regions it even serves as a residential fuel for heating and cooking. Coal with special properties, known as coking coal, is a crucial input into steelmaking. One major part of the energy landscape where coal no longer has a significant role is transportation, with oil-based fuels now providing over 90% of the energy needed.

Coal's low cost has been a significant part of its appeal, as has the energy security it is believed to bring. After two oil shocks in the 1970s, oil-consuming countries made a

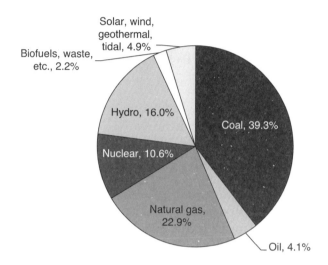

**Figure 1.1** Global gross electricity production by source, 2015

*Source:* IEA, *Electricity Information 2017*

conscious choice to deepen their reliance on coal-fired electric power plants as a bulwark against the perceived power of oil-exporting countries. (Oil used to be a more important fuel for power generation than it is today.) Today, roughly 85% of developed countries generate significant electricity with coal.[2] In many of these countries, coal accounts for a large share of overall power generation – for example, 61% in Australia, 46% in South Korea, 37% in Germany, 34% in Japan, and 31% in the United States as of 2017.[3] Coal is even bigger in major developing nations, with China and India relying on coal for 67% and 76% of their electricity, respectively.[4]

World coal consumption grew massively in the 2000s, mainly because of a huge expansion of coal-fired power capacity in China (see Figure 1.2). From 2000 through 2013, China turned itself into the world's manufacturing

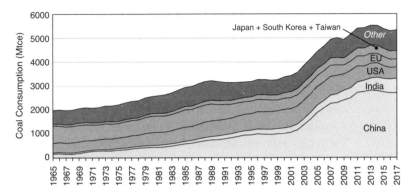

**Figure 1.2** World coal consumption, including thermal and coking coal, in million tonnes of coal equivalent (Mtce) (Mtce is an energy unit that normalizes tonnage of coal by the energy value of the coal)

*Source:* BP Statistical Review of World Energy 2018

powerhouse and boosted per capita GDP sevenfold in the process – an achievement made possible in part by a nearly threefold increase in coal production and consumption.[5] India's coal consumption has also grown steadily, and other developing countries are following China's and India's lead in ramping up coal-fired power capacity (see Figure 1.2).

Now, we may be at an inflection point when it comes to coal. China's massive coal expansion is over, which contributed to an overall drop in global coal use in 2015 and 2016. Whether coal consumption in China has peaked for good is not entirely clear – it ticked up slightly in 2017 – but China's government is trying to put the brakes on further growth in coal use. Coal is in terminal decline in North America, a victim mainly of the shale gas revolution, which has caused natural gas to supplant coal as the preferred energy source in the power sector. Other developed countries – notably Germany, Japan, and South Korea – have continued to lean on coal-fired power plants in recent years, but the appetite for further growth has cooled.

The big question going forward is what happens in countries that are still in an earlier phase of development than China. India plans to expand coal production and use even as it seeks to significantly increase wind and solar capacity. Other countries in South Asia (Pakistan and Bangladesh) and Southeast Asia (especially Indonesia, Vietnam, the Philippines, and Malaysia) are building long-lived new coal power plants at a rapid pace. Beyond these fast-growing economies, the next wave of countries hoping to develop still appear to view coal as their "default fuel." The energy choices of countries on the steep part of the economic development curve will determine whether the global coal consumption trajectory shown in Figure 1.2 continues to go down, plateaus, or starts trending up again.

## Coal's environmental problems

From the start, coal has brought environmental problems alongside prosperity. Smog from coal combustion was offending Londoners as far back as the 1300s.[6] Today, respiratory disease associated with air pollution from coal is responsible for hundreds of thousands of premature deaths per year, especially in developing Asia. Coal mine accidents, illnesses affecting miners, and mine-related environmental damage remain significant problems in mining regions. People who don't directly experience health, safety, or air quality impacts from coal may be concerned about its massive emissions of carbon dioxide ($CO_2$), a long-lived greenhouse gas.

It is little surprise that discussions around coal – including those in this book – are polarizing. Environmentalists may bristle at the suggestion that coal should have any role at all in the energy system, given its environmental downsides. Those working in the coal sector – or planning energy policy in fast-growing countries – may bristle at the implication that the benefits of economic growth, which coal has played a role in providing, are not an equally important factor to take into account.

It is not the purpose of this book to render a verdict on whether the benefits coal has brought have exceeded its costs, or whether they will in the future. Nor is the goal to forecast how long it will be until global coal use peaks. As we have learned from the shale gas revolution in the United States, or from the unexpectedly rapid decreases in the costs of renewable energy worldwide, energy markets are dynamic and likely to surprise.

The goal of this book, instead, is to explain the basic economic and political dynamics that will shape coal's future. Why does coal play such an important role in today's energy system? What are the political conflicts on local, national, and international levels that will influence policies affecting coal? What would it take for other energy sources to outcompete coal in the marketplace?

## The nature of energy resources

In order to address our questions about coal, we first need to understand some fundamental characteristics of energy resources. A good starting point is the recognition that energy is not an end product. What the final consumer actually cares about is *energy services*. As an individual, I want energy to drive a car, or to watch television, or to have light at night. As a business owner, I want energy to run machines on my manufacturing line, or to provide air conditioning that keeps my employees (and computer servers) cool, or to cook the food I am selling. I want these energy services to be there when I need them, to have minimal undesirable side effects (for example, my stove shouldn't fill the restaurant with smoke), and to be as cheap as possible. But apart from that – and apart from any broader social or environmental concerns I might have as a citizen – I don't care where my energy comes from. Whether my stove runs on electricity or natural gas or propane is largely unimportant to me as a consumer. So is whether the electrons flowing out of the socket on my wall were generated by a coal-fired power plant or a wind turbine or a hydroelectric dam.

Since demand for energy is a derived demand, meaning that it comes from demand for energy-using applications, any energy source can in theory compete with any other energy source that is able to provide the same services. All else equal, markets will supply consumers with the cheapest energy. Where fossil fuels are concerned, this phenomenon of "BTU arbitrage" (BTU, for British Thermal Unit, is a measure of energy) has traditionally favored coal (see Figure 1.3). More than anything else, coal's low cost and wide geographical distribution explain why it is the dominant fuel for electricity generation around the world, as well as an important source of energy for industrial applications. (Oil-based fuels have the dominant role in transportation because of their higher energy density and easier transportability, while natural gas is more easily piped into dense residential areas as a fuel for heating and cooking.)

Energy resources decline in importance because alternatives emerge that are cheaper and/or better suited to supplying the energy services desired. The same will be true for coal. Whether the world still uses significant quantities of coal decades from now will depend on how competitive coal remains with other energy sources. Interfuel competition is shaped by three main factors: resource depletion,

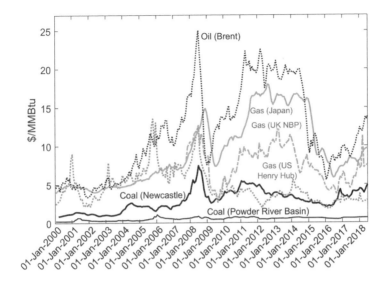

**Figure 1.3** Coal, natural gas, and oil prices compared on an energy basis (Powder River Basin coal prices are at mine mouth)

*Source:* IHS McCloskey, Bloomberg

technological change, and policy. These factors interact with each other.

Resource depletion is often misunderstood. As we will discuss further in Chapter 2, depletion does *not* mean we will ever run out of coal – or any other energy resource, for that matter. What does happen is that more geologically favorable deposits are mined first. In the absence of improvements in mining methods, this would cause production costs to increase over time, making coal less competitive against alternatives.

In reality, technological change means that mining methods *do* improve. If technological improvements outpace the effects of mine depletion, production costs can go down over time. The same is true, of course, of other means of producing energy, which makes the competition between energy sources very dynamic. For example, the shale gas revolution in the United States was driven by the innovation of combining three technologies: hydraulic fracturing to let natural gas flow in relatively non-porous rock, horizontal drilling to economically collect gas from thin shale layers, and advanced seismic imaging to show where the gas was likely to be. These technologies resulted in significant decreases in the cost of producing natural gas, which in turn gave gas an edge over coal for electricity generation in the US.

Government policy affects interfuel competition in numerous ways, including by affecting the cost of producing and using different kinds of energy. When it comes to coal, environmental policy is the most important kind of policy affecting the fuel's competitiveness relative to alternatives. Burning coal results in a number of what economists call "negative externalities" – costs to society that aren't paid by those using the coal. If these negative externalities were more widely and fully incorporated into the price of coal – for example through a tax on emissions of local pollutants or greenhouse gases – coal would become relatively less competitive against alternatives.

Most governments do not regulate the environmental attributes of energy production and consumption as much as environmentalists think they should. In richer countries, coal burning is usually subject to controls on the emissions that cause local air pollution, such as sulfur oxides ($SO_x$), nitrogen oxides ($NO_x$), and particulates. Even among rich countries though, there are rarely strong policies to address greenhouse gas emissions, in part because the impacts of climate change are less directly visible and in part because the technologies to reduce these emissions are expensive. In developing countries, even basic air quality regulation tends to be at a nascent stage. Usually there is pressure to grow the economy and meet citizens' basic needs – for jobs, for safety, for security – before there is significant pressure to clean the air, although worsening air pollution can certainly bring environmental concerns to the fore in short order. Even when governments start to be responsive to the environmental concerns of a growing middle class, it can take time for them to develop the institutional capability to effectively regulate pollution.

## Factors shaping the future of coal

Today, coal is both dominant and under threat. As discussed above, it is the backbone of power grids for much of the world, and it remains, for the moment, the seeming default choice for energy among countries seeking to rapidly expand their power grids and grow their economies. Existing coal reserves are estimated to be adequate for over 100 years.[7]

At the same time, China, the world's largest producer and consumer of coal by far, is actively seeking to limit its future coal use. China, India, and many other countries are grappling with serious air pollution problems that have significant contributions from coal. And international environmental organizations are targeting coal due to its outsize carbon dioxide emissions.

The tensions around coal play out in the political arena at local, national, and international levels. At the local level, coal brings jobs, economic activity, and tax revenue (as well as, sometimes, corrupt payments). As a result, local or state governments may look the other way when small mines disobey government edicts to close or when coal-using enterprises flout air pollution rules and keep running. At the same time, coal's heaviest burdens often fall on local communities, in the form, for example, of accidents or respiratory diseases affecting miners, pollution of water, or disturbance of the landscape from mining.

Coal can be a flashpoint in national politics, where coal-producing and coal-using enterprises may be influential. The financial sector can be tied to coal as well. For example, state-owned banks in China and India are significant enough creditors to coal mines or coal-fired power plants that a rapid shift away from coal might threaten them. At the electoral level, coal regions can carry weight in national elections even when coal sector employment is low as a share of overall national employment. Many coal regions have been disrupted by productivity improvements in coal mining, which have reduced the number of available mining jobs. (In the US, cheap natural gas has been another source of job loss in the coal sector.) Blaming the loss of coal livelihoods on excessive environmental concern instead of market forces and technological change can be an effective political tactic.

Countries have often sought to expand coal production and consumption as a way to ensure their energy security. China restructured its coal institutions multiple times over several decades to remove bottlenecks to coal production and economic growth. The United States and Japan aggressively pushed coal for power generation starting in the late 1970s. India hopes to expand its domestic coal production to reduce dependence on imports.

At the international level, the politics around coal track closely with the politics around climate change. International environmental organizations treat coal as environmental enemy #1, and the climate change focus of their advocacy is evident from their push for coal's complete elimination, as opposed to the installation of technologies for controlling local emissions. At the behest of the developed country governments that fund it, the World Bank has indicated it will largely eschew financing for new coal power stations on environmental grounds.[8] At the same time, many developed countries continue to burn substantial coal themselves, and they have not offered clear alternatives to coal to countries hoping to expand their power-generating capacity – countries whose GDP per capita and greenhouse gas emissions per capita are typically far lower than their own.

Each of the main alternatives to coal has specific disadvantages beyond cost alone. Renewables like wind and solar require management of intermittency – the fact that power is only available when the wind is blowing or the sun is shining. Natural gas requires the development of costly transportation infrastructure and a reliable, financially viable value chain from gas field to end user. Nuclear power plants are costly to build and unpopular almost everywhere, which can lead to major regulatory delays and associated cost overruns. Hydro and geothermal are highly site-specific.

The future outlook for coal depends on the pace of both technological change and policy change, which in turn depend on how governments prioritize economic and environmental considerations in response to pressure from their constituents. Aggressive policy action on climate change will tend to shorten the lifetime of coal. Relatively weak climate policy, such as the world has mostly pursued thus far, will extend the amount of time coal remains a major global energy resource.

In the remainder of the book, I review the political, economic, and technological factors that have shaped coal's past and will shape its future. Countries have most often turned to coal because they perceive it to be "energy secure" – cheap and readily available over the long term. Chapter 2 describes how this energy security logic has spurred coal adoption historically – from Britain's original embrace of the fuel as a substitute for wood-based energy to power industrial development, to the conscious adoption of coal by developed countries starting in the late 1970s as a substitute for oil in electricity generation, to China's coal-fueled industrial expansion in the 1990s and 2000s, to the present-day build-outs of coal-fired power capacity that have continued apace in South Asia and Southeast Asia. The energy security rationale for coal remains valid in the sense that the world is not running out of cheap coal. However, uncertainty around coal's continued environmental accept-ability has the potential to make the fuel less energy secure than it might seem.

As discussed in Chapter 3, coal's relatively robust value chain has helped make it a fuel of choice. Coal can be mined with fairly rudimentary technology, which has allowed small, inefficient, and sometimes unsafe mines to exist alongside highly mechanized modern ones. Coal can be transported by railroads, barges, or trucks, giving it a market advantage over natural gas, with its requirement for expensive, specialized transportation infrastructure. Coal can be burned in simple boilers as well as modern ultra-supercritical power plants. Still, there are tensions along the coal value chain that play out at local, national, and international levels. The most fundamental tension is between economic benefits and environmental qual-ity. National governments trying to improve air quality may find themselves stymied by coal-producing and coal-consuming interests that are supported by subnational governments for the local economic benefits they bring. The interests of coal producers and coal consumers (most often power companies) can themselves conflict, especially in countries like China and India where there is significant government ownership and intervention in both the coal and power sectors – and where different levels of government may be aligned with different parts of the coal value chain. Monopoly rail networks may constrain coal shipments and increase delivered prices. Environmental organizations may try to exploit frictions in the coal value chain as a strategy for diminishing the role of coal.

Environmental policymaking will play a particularly important role in shaping coal's future, and it is considered in detail in Chapter 4. Simple theories of environmental regulation suggest that environmental problems receive more attention after citizens' basic needs are met, and also that locally salient environmental impacts like air pollution are a stronger spur to regulation than global concerns like climate change. Even in rich countries, strong policy action to reduce greenhouse gas emissions has been relatively rare. The future trajectory of coal will depend importantly on whether the appetite for stringent climate policy grows in the future. Environmental groups have tried to diminish the public acceptability of coal, push coal alternatives, and directly fight coal in various venues, but thus far their efforts have had only mixed success.

Technological advancements have the potential to minimize the environmental impact of coal use, for example through the use of carbon capture and storage (CCS). Technological change could also make alternatives to coal economically attractive enough that coal becomes less dominant purely through market forces (especially if markets start to price in environmental externalities). Chapter 5 considers the prospects for "clean coal technologies" as well as coal alternatives, with a focus on nuclear power, natural gas, and renewables. The chapter does not attempt to predict if and when coal will be replaced; rather, its goal is to explain the strengths and weaknesses of the available energy supply alternatives in comparison to coal – and what technological advancements might shift the balance in one way or another.

Chapter 6 concludes with a discussion of how environmental policy and technological change could shape the role of coal going forward. Coal has been inextricably tied to industrial development for over 200 years. How long this will continue to be the case will depend on the factors discussed in this book.

## Conclusion

Coal is the energy source that ushered in the industrial age, and it still sustains it in many countries around the world today. In 2015, coal produced 28% of the world's primary energy, and it plays a particularly important role in the power sector, where it produced 39% of the world's electricity, the most of any energy source. Coal is especially dominant in large emerging markets like China and India, but a number of large developed economies – including the United States, Germany, Japan, and South Korea – also lean on it for a significant share of electricity generation. Growth in coal use has tailed off in most developed countries – and possibly in China as well – but many emerging economies still view coal as important to their energy futures and continue to build long-lived new coal-fired power plants.

Coal's low cost and wide availability compared with other energy sources have made it popular, but coal has always brought serious health and environmental problems with it. Smog from coal burning was a problem in 1300s London, and air pollution from coal today causes hundreds of thousands of premature deaths around the world, especially in the smog-choked metropolises of developing Asia. Climate change is a problem that is longer term and less immediately visible, but concerns about the high greenhouse gas emissions footprint of coal have produced significant pressure from international organizations and some developed country governments for coal use to be curtailed around the world.

The future of coal will be shaped by the tension between coal's perceived value as a low-cost, "energy secure" fuel and the effort to reduce (or eliminate) its key role in the global energy system because of its environmental negatives. This tension will play out at local, national, and international levels. Local communities can be major beneficiaries of coal in terms of jobs and economic activity. They can also bear the largest burdens of coal production and use, for example from mining-related accidents and illnesses, air and water pollution, and loss of non-coal-connected livelihoods. At the national level, coal producing and consuming interests square off against environmental groups fighting coal through every available stakeholder process. In countries from the US to India, coal regions may be electorally significant even where coal employment is not enormous as a share of national employment. The international politics around coal can pit environmental groups seeking to eliminate coal use against developing country policymakers who believe they need coal to grow their economies and lift their citizens out of poverty.

The rest of this book explores in detail the factors that will determine how long coal continues to be a major part of the global energy system. Chapter 2 traces the history of how different countries have turned to coal to secure their energy futures, from Britain's exploitation of coal to fuel the Industrial Revolution, to developed countries, emphasis on coal starting in the late 1970s as a way to reduce their dependence on oil, to China's massive coal-backed industrialization and dependence growth in the 2000s. It considers whether the "energy security" rationale for coal still holds in a world increasingly concerned about climate change. Chapter 3 lays out the entire coal value chain from mining, to transportation by rail or road or ship, to end use in power plants or industrial boilers or blast furnaces. There can be conflicts along the coal value chain, for example between the coal and power sectors, but there are also strong interests that resist any reduction in coal's role, like locally operated mines, powerful coal-consuming industries, and financial players that have a heavy investment in coal. Chapter 4 examines the critical role environmental policy will play in determining coal's future. In the developing countries where coal use is growing, it is likely that air pollution will be a nearer-term prod toward environmental regulations that affect coal, but longer term, coal's future may depend more on the trajectory of climate policy around the world. Chapter 5 describes various possible energy supply alternatives that are cleaner than conventional coal burning, from wind and solar to nuclear to natural gas to coal-fired power plants that capture carbon dioxide to avoid climate change impact. At the moment, all of these alternatives have disadvantages beyond cost alone, but they are likely to improve over time, especially if supported by environmental and technology policies. Chapter 6 concludes with an overall look at where coal might go from here, with a focus on the technology innovations and country-level policies that could make coal more or less attractive in the future.

# CHAPTER TWO

# The Quest for Energy Security

## Coal: the first source of (nearly) unlimited energy

If energy security means having reliable access to ample quantities of energy at an affordable price, coal was the first fuel in history to provide energy security on an industrial scale. Before the widespread use of coal, human activities were constrained by the energy available from trees or water. Water availability was site-specific, and dependence on trees for wood and charcoal caused serious deforestation. By making available the concentrated energy from prehistoric plant matter (see Box 2.1),[1] coal provided humankind with its first energy source that was, for all practical purposes, unlimited.

---

**Box 2.1** The origin and characteristics of coal

Coal is a combustible rock that is the product of ancient plant matter that did not decay fully and was compressed and heated under the earth over time. The properties of a particular coal vary widely depending on the geological conditions that formed it. Most of the largest coal deposits around the world have their origin in the Carboniferous period, which lasted from about 359 to 299 million years ago. The Carboniferous period was notable for huge warm swamps. When plant matter of

---

all kinds sank beneath stagnant, oxygen-poor water, it did not decay completely, instead turning into energy-rich peat. Over time, this peat could end up being buried deeper and deeper in sediment. Moisture would be squeezed out, and the high temperatures and pressures at depth would speed up chemical reactions that released $H_2O$, $CO_2$, and $CH_4$. The carbon became more concentrated, and the peat was transformed into coal.

Coal "rank" is a function largely (though not entirely) of the depth at which the peat was buried, and thus the temperatures to which it was exposed. The lowest-rank coals, which are typically found closest to the surface and were exposed to temperatures less than 100°C during formation, are lignites or brown coals. They have the lowest carbon and energy content among coals and the highest moisture fraction. Sub-bituminous coal is the next highest rank, followed by bituminous, and finally anthracite. Anthracite is the coal that saw the highest temperatures (around 200°C) during formation. It has the highest carbon and energy content and the lowest moisture fraction.

In addition to moisture and energy content, coals are typically characterized by their volatile matter (compounds other than water – mainly hydrocarbons – that are released at medium high temperatures in the absence of oxygen), ash content (non-burnable minerals), and sulfur content. High ash is undesirable, as it means less energy and more residue after combustion, and generally more particulate pollution. Sulfur is undesirable as well because it leads to the formation of $SO_2$ when the coal is burned.

Coking coal, also known as metallurgical (or "met") coal, is coal with specific properties that make it suitable for making iron and steel. Coking coal is converted into the nearly pure-carbon "coke" used to produce the pig iron that is then turned into steel. Coking coal is generally bituminous, low-ash, and low-sulfur.

Thermal coal (or steam coal, so-called because its typical purpose is to generate steam in a boiler for heat or electricity generation) refers to any coal that is not coking coal or lignite.

Great Britain was the pioneer of large-scale coal utilization and coal production. An important driver was the dwindling availability of firewood. In the 1560s, coal produced approximately 24% of the portion of Britain's energy that didn't come from animal or human power; by the beginning of the 1700s, the figure was 77%.[2] In the late 1700s, coal helped catalyze the Industrial Revolution. As Barbara Freese recounts in her book *Coal: A Human History*, coal production, ironmaking, the steam engine, and new techniques of mass production all reinforced each other, helping to give industrialization its unstoppable momentum.[3] The steam engine pumped water out of mines to increase coal production. Coal-fired steam locomotives transported coal long distances over land. Iron was smelted with "coke" made from coal instead of scarce charcoal, and the bellows that fanned the flame were run with a coal-powered steam engine instead of a waterwheel. Iron became steam engines, railroads, factories, and the machines inside them. In short, coal helped bring into existence the industrial capability that makes modern life possible.

The energy transition from wood to coal took place over many years, at different paces, around the world. Globally, coal was about 5% of the world energy market in 1840, and 50% in 1900. Whereas coal had already eclipsed wood as an energy source in Britain by the start of the 1700s, wood didn't start to fade quickly in Germany and France until after 1850, and wood persisted as a major energy source in Russia, Italy, and Spain into the twentieth century.[4] Coal mining started to take off in the United States in the middle of the 1800s, and by 1900 US output surpassed that of the UK.[5] (The US ceded the top spot in coal production on a raw tonnage basis to China in 1985.)

## Coal as the OECD's antidote to oil insecurity

Oil emerged as a major new energy source in the late nineteenth century, with initial use as an illuminant that was superior to existing alternatives. In the early twentieth century, electric lighting supplanted oil lamps, but around the same time oil found the application that is still its most important today, as a fuel for motor vehicles.[6] Liquid fuels refined from oil could readily be transported via pipeline for use in filling stations. Oil could also be used for electricity generation. In the 1960s, low oil prices and environmental considerations spurred increasing use of fuel oil as a substitute for coal in power plants.[7] Coal may have been good for power generation and heating, but oil was good for power generation, heating, *and* transportation.

However, oil-consuming nations experienced a rude awakening when the Organization of Arab Petroleum Exporting Countries declared an oil embargo in October 1973 to protest US support of Israel in the Yom Kippur War. Suddenly, heavy reliance on oil no longer seemed like such a good idea. The member countries of the Organization for Economic Co-operation and Development (OECD) founded the International Energy Agency (IEA) in 1974 to coordinate with each other in an effort to reduce vulnerability to future oil shocks.

Another oil shock came soon enough, in 1979, the result

of global panic and decreased output following the Iranian Revolution. In response, the IEA decided that a key pillar of energy security should be substitution of oil with coal wherever possible. Substitution for oil in transportation wasn't straightforward; the power sector offered lower-hanging fruit. Coal was already the leading fuel for electric power at the time, responsible for about one-third of the world's generation, but oil wasn't that far behind, with roughly a 20% share, similar to hydro.[8]

The "Principles for IEA Action on Coal" that the IEA adopted in May 1979 called for "enlarged coal use, primarily through minimizing the use of oil in electricity generation and encouraging the construction of new coal-fired power plants."[9] The principles called for IEA member countries to expand their production of coal, and specifically noted the potential for Australia, Canada, and the United States to expand both their production and export capability. The IEA hoped that expanding coal production and trade around the world could help de-link energy security from oil, at least when it came to power generation.

In a detailed and thoughtful 1979 article in *Foreign Affairs*, the IEA's first executive director, Ulf Lantzke, expressed an energy-security-based rationale for expanding coal use. In essence, he argued that global oil production, and in particular OPEC oil production, would not be able to keep pace with demand, and that, in the absence of alternatives, "closing the gap" would entail reduced economic growth on the part of oil-consuming countries. (While Lantzke's article is generally well argued, he does at times fall victim to the "peak oil" fallacy; this notion that we might hit some constraining "peak" in oil, coal, or anything else is critiqued later in this chapter.) Lantzke noted that China and the Soviet Union already derived about 50% of their energy from coal, whereas the figure was only 20% for the OECD countries.

Even in 1979, it was understood that a massive expansion of coal production and use could possibly trade an energy security problem for a climate one.[10] As Lantzke put it in the article:

> A possible longer term and more profound objection to increased reliance on energy from fossil fuel combustion (not just coal combustion) is doubt about the inherent ability of the earth's environment to absorb and recycle the carbon dioxide produced, and about the consequent effect on the earth's climate.
>
> The amount of carbon dioxide in the atmosphere has steadily increased from about 313 ppmv (particles per million by volume) in 1958 to 334 ppmv in 1978. Continuing increase might cause a "greenhouse effect" by altering the radiation balance of the atmosphere. A global temperature increase and major climatic changes might result.
>
> Ulf Lantzke (1979), "Expanding world use of coal,"
> *Foreign Affairs* 58(2).

Lantzke went on to argue that knowledge at the time didn't justify shying away from coal, but that climate change was an important concern to continue studying – and presumably responding to, if the accumulation of more scientific knowledge showed the threat to be real and serious:

> $CO_2$ production from greatly increased coal consumption may turn out to be a long-term problem if coal use were likely to continue indefinitely at high rates. So far, the evidence [as of 1979! – author] seems too weak to prevent coal from playing a major part in the energy supply over the next fifty years, but there is a continual need for careful study of the level of carbon dioxide and for the acquisition of knowledge of the mechanism involved in $CO_2$ transfer.
>
> Ulf Lantzke (1979), "Expanding world use of coal,"
> *Foreign Affairs* 58(2).

The OECD's deliberate push into coal was a success. Between 1980 and 2000, OECD countries increased their use of coal in electricity generation by over 60% while decreasing their use of oil for that purpose by about 40%.[11] This "dash to coal" contributed to the expansion of the seaborne trade in steam coal for power generation by more than a factor of four.[12] Japan's demand for coal played a particularly important role in catalyzing the development of the coal industries of South Africa, Australia, and, later, Indonesia.

Even before the oil panic, Japan had started to import significant quantities of coking coal to feed its rapidly growing steel industry, which by 1970 was the world's third-largest producer of steel. A 1971 contract for South African coal producers to supply Japanese steel mills with coking coal helped drive a significant expansion of South Africa's coal industry.[13] Japan was also a key early export customer for Australian coal – initially coking coal, but later, after the oil crisis, steam coal as well.[14] Later, Indonesia's coal industry was established, based on the prospect of coal exports to Japan especially, but also to South Korea and Taiwan, which like Japan had few energy resources of their own.[15] (Energy security concerns also encouraged the Japanese government to underwrite early liquefied natural gas export projects from Indonesia in the 1970s.)[16] Coal demand from Northeast Asia provided a long-term, reliable revenue source that drew investment to the coal industries of South Africa, Australia, and Indonesia. Without this demand, it is doubtful these three countries' coal sectors would have grown as quickly as they did.

Coal is still a major energy source in the OECD. The United States remains the largest coal user among developed countries in absolute terms, though coal's role in the US has shrunk significantly due to cheap natural gas. In

Asia, Japan, South Korea, and Taiwan have continued to rely heavily on coal. In Europe, Germany and Poland have done the same. The common thread is energy security concerns.

Japan's energy security situation became much more urgent with the shutdown of nuclear capacity following the Fukushima accident in 2011 – and the slow and uncertain path to bringing reactors back online since then. The country has responded with energy conservation measures and also by ramping up electricity generation from natural gas and coal.[17] Japan has ramped up renewable generation too, but from a low base, and with a much smaller contribution to generation.

Like Japan, South Korea and Taiwan are geographically isolated and have very limited energy resources of their own, which has made them sensitive to energy security and willing to prioritize coal. Still, this has not made coal immune to controversy. Following his election in May 2017, South Korean president Moon Jae-in caused jitters in Asian coal markets and South Korea's power sector when he pledged to shut down existing coal plants and halt the construction of new ones.[18] At the time of writing, it remained unclear exactly what this pledge would mean for the future of coal in South Korea, but at the very least it shows that coal is subject to challenge even in countries acutely concerned about security of energy supply.

Germany has been drastically reducing its nuclear generation due to deep anti-nuclear sentiment there, especially since Fukushima. Germany has relied heavily on coal-fired power capacity to fill the gap left by the closure of nuclear units. Natural gas could play a bigger role in Germany in theory, but in practice it has not been prioritized. A combination of factors favor coal in Germany, including the political heft of domestic coal interests and concerns about high gas prices and over-reliance on pipeline gas from Russia.

Poland produces even more coal than Germany – and is even more coal-dependent for power. As of early 2018, Poland's government was still planning for 50% of its electricity in 2050 to come from coal.[19] Poland leans on coal not only because of the political influence of mining regions, but also because coal is perceived as an energy security bulwark against dependence on Russian natural gas.

One part of the world where coal use is shrinking fast is North America. The largest single reason for this is that the shale gas revolution in North America has driven down the price of natural gas, making gas-fired power plants a cheaper way to generate electricity than coal-fired ones.[20] Increasing renewable generation, flat electricity demand, and the possibility of tighter environmental rules in the future also make any expansions of coal-fired electricity generation in North America unlikely.

## China's coal-based energy security paradigm

Coal development was given high priority from the founding of the People's Republic of China in 1949. Under the Soviet-style system of central planning, coal production was consolidated in state-owned mines controlled at the central and local levels, and the coal from these mines was provided at low price to heavy industry, which the central government wanted to boost. The coal sector grew rapidly in the 1950s, but by the 1970s, the fundamental flaws of central planning had become all too apparent. Low, administratively determined coal prices created insufficient incentives for production, and the lack of competition removed any drive for innovation and efficiency improvement. By the late 1970s, electricity shortages caused by insufficient coal had become a serious brake on the economy.

China's government was so concerned about lack of energy holding back the economy that it was willing to go against its strongly ingrained central planning instincts in order to expand the coal supply. The government encouraged greater participation by town and village enterprise (TVE) mines and allowed market pricing for some coal. This began the several-decades-long transformation of China's coal sector that has led to the mostly market-driven coal industry of today (a contrast to the power sector, which has retained a heavier degree of state involvement and intervention).[21]

Just as in the OECD countries, China's focus on coal has important roots in perceived oil insecurity – as well as broader anxiety about import dependence. China's sensitivities around oil took shape even earlier than in the OECD nations. China was heavily dependent on the Soviet Union for oil expertise and oil products through the 1950s, and it suffered heavily when Soviet support was withdrawn in 1960 due to a deterioration in relations between the two countries.[22] Through a concerted effort at domestic exploration and production, China regained oil self-sufficiency, becoming a net exporter in 1970.[23] However, insatiable demand from its racing economy turned it into a net oil importer again in 1993, which refocused policymakers yet again on shoring up domestic coal output.[24] US military interventions in the Middle East, and concerns that the US Navy could block oil shipping routes in a conflict, also informed China's perceptions about oil security. (It can be argued that China's powerful national oil companies had their own vested interest in oil being treated as a matter of special national security, including because it helped them expand their operations abroad.)[25] China's efforts at boost-

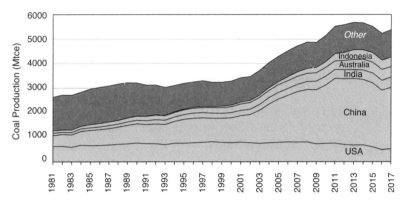

**Figure 2.1** World coal production, including thermal and coking coal, in million tonnes of coal equivalent (Mtce) (Mtce is an energy unit that normalizes tonnage of coal by the energy value of the coal)

*Source:* BP Statistical Review of World Energy 2018

ing domestic coal production since the 1990s have been extremely successful, leading to the fastest absolute growth in coal output the world has even seen (see Figure 2.1).

Even today, the energy security rationale colors a range of technology and policy choices touching on coal in China. It's at least one factor behind China's contemplated ban on cars running on (largely imported) fossil fuels, though local pollution reduction and the search for industrial advantage are two other powerful motivations.[26] (If coal continues to be used to generate a large share of electricity in China, switching to electric vehicles will not necessarily reduce greenhouse gas emissions from transportation.)

The importance of energy security considerations is also illustrated by the way that carbon capture and storage (CCS) in China is being developed most aggressively for use with coal conversion processes that could produce useful liquid and gaseous fuels. China has been experimenting with technologies for carbon capture and storage (CCS) since the 2000s,[27] and a wave of new project announcements was seen by some as signifying that China had become the epicenter of CCS development.[28] The basic idea of CCS technology, as discussed in Chapter 5, is to capture the $CO_2$ from combustion and store it underground to prevent its release to the atmosphere. Given the huge $CO_2$ footprint of China's fleet of coal power plants, development of CCS in China might seem like a sign of the country's seriousness in trying to reduce greenhouse gas emissions. The pattern of actual progress, however, shows energy security motives to be a more important driver of China's CCS efforts than climate concern per se. The CCS projects that have advanced the fastest are attached to technologies that would also enhance energy security. State-owned coal giant Shenhua has demonstrated capture and storage of $CO_2$ from a coal-to-liquids (CTL) process that turns coal into a liquid fuel that could substitute for oil in transportation. Shaanxi Yanchang Petroleum Group announced a project to convert coal into a gas that could substitute for natural gas, with $CO_2$ from the process being captured and pumped into oilfields for enhanced oil recovery (EOR), a technique for boosting oil production from mature fields.[29] Making alternative liquid and gaseous fuels from coal has the potential to reduce China's import dependence, as does boosting domestic oil production by using $CO_2$ for EOR.

By contrast, adding CCS to coal-fired power plants could degrade China's energy security rather than enhancing it, as energy researchers Richard Morse, Varun Rai, and Gang He have pointed out.[30] This is true for several reasons. First, capturing the dilute stream of $CO_2$ from coal power plant exhaust adds much more cost than capturing it from the kinds of coal conversion processes described above, which produce more concentrated streams of $CO_2$. CCS has the potential to add 40% or more to the cost of coal power.[31] Implementing CCS at scale in China for conventional coal-fired power would therefore mean paying significantly more for electricity, and yet the government has traditionally prioritized keeping power prices low to stimulate growth and contain inflation. Second, around 20% of a conventional coal-fired power plant's energy would likely be needed to operate the CCS process itself, which means burning that much more coal. This would put more stress on the coal value chain. Given China's focus on energy security, we should not be surprised that this has made CCS for coal power less attractive than CCS developments focused on coal conversion and EOR. Coal is considered energy-secure because of its availability and low cost. Technologies and policies that stress coal supply and increase cost erode these advantages.

For all its historical focus on coal as the foundation of energy security, China's government is well aware of the negative environmental externalities of the fuel. It also recognizes that overdependence on coal is not desirable from an energy security perspective. In the 2016–2020 Five-Year Plan, China laid out the goal of capping coal consumption at 4.1 billion tonnes and reducing coal's share of primary energy to 58 percent by 2020 (from 64 percent in 2015).[32] The country is expanding the share of wind and solar, nuclear power, and natural-gas-fired power in the electricity mix at a rapid rate. That said, non-coal resources other than hydro start from low shares in the current generation mix, and the US Energy Information Administration predicted in 2017 that coal would still supply almost 50% of electricity in China in 2040.[33] (Some argue that forecasts from both the US Energy Information Administration and the International Energy Agency have historically been too pessimistic about technological improvements in coal alternatives.)

## Coal and energy security in India

Like China, India views coal as crucial to its energy security. Absolute coal use is expected to grow more in India
than any other country between now and 2040. India's
per capita GDP is less than half of China's, and its carbon
emissions are less than a fourth of China's (and roughly
a tenth those of the United States). India's government is
understandably reluctant to do anything that would constrain economic growth and keep it from lifting millions of
its citizens out of poverty. This has historically translated
into a hard-line position at the climate negotiating table,
especially when it comes to resisting any kind of carbon cap
that might curtail the country's use of coal.[34]

India's national policymakers, like China's, retain a bias
toward central planning. However, they have had more
difficulty than China's policymakers in implementing
pragmatic, flexible policies in the coal and power sectors to
address problems resulting from central planning. Reasons
for this include complex legal and social issues around land
ownership and land acquisition, the dominance of government-owned Coal India Limited and the government rail
monopoly, and the fact that electricity distribution entities
at the state level mostly lose money. Some reforms aimed
at boosting domestic coal production have been moderately effective (for example, the restructuring and partial
privatization of Coal India Limited, the introduction of
"e-auctions" of market-priced coal, and the opening of coal
production to "captive" mining), but they have not been
enough to stave off the growing need for coal imports,
which served almost 30% of India's coal demand in 2015.[35]
Self-sufficiency in coal remains one of India's foremost
objectives for energy policy, reflecting the government's
perception that domestic coal is more energy secure.[36]

## Coal and energy security in other developing countries

Based on the pipeline of coal power plant construction as tracked by Coalswarm, the Sierra Club, and Greenpeace,[37] most developing countries that want to significantly expand their electricity-generating capacity still appear to see coal as their go-to option for energy security. The populous, fast-growing economies of Southeast Asia are a particular hot spot for coal. Indonesia, with its ample reserves of low-rank coal, initiated a "fast track" program in 2006 to build out coal-fired power plants.[38] Though many of these projects have fallen behind their original schedules, Indonesia continues to add coal-fired units at a rapid pace. Vietnam has even larger amounts of coal-fired power capacity currently under construction.[39] The Philippines and Malaysia also have significant coal-fired capacity under construction and in the planning stages. South Asia is seeing growth in coal use beyond India, with Pakistan adding significant capacity and Bangladesh planning to.[40] Bangladesh used to rely on cheap natural gas from domestic fields, but low gas prices encouraged consumption and discouraged investment in supply, to the point where coal is now viewed as a more energy-secure option.

At the same time as they turn to coal, many of these countries are wrestling with the tension between energy security and environmental objectives. For example, Vietnam's national energy blueprint as of 2015 envisioned a massive expansion of coal-fired capacity, but the government announced plans in early 2016 to rely more heavily on natural gas, nuclear, and renewables, though growth in coal-fired power is still expected.[41] Coal power projects are facing increasing opposition around the world.

A longer-term question is whether the next wave of

economic development around the world will also be propelled by coal. Many of the lowest-income countries have poorly developed central electricity grids. Many are also heavily reliant on hydropower. When water levels are high, hydro is cheap, and it can also be a perfect backup for wind and solar power. For example, Ethiopia has the highest fraction of intermittent renewable generation of any low-income country with a significant grid, with about 4% of its generation coming from wind,[42] and this high wind penetration is enabled in part by the hydropower that supplies almost all of the rest of Ethiopia's electricity. (The highest intermittent renewable fraction in the electricity production mix of any country, rich or poor, is greater than 40%, in Denmark, which generates large amounts of energy from wind.) From an energy security perspective, however, hydro is a double-edged sword. Often the cheapest, most readily available hydro resources have been tapped already, so there are limited prospects for expanding hydropower to keep pace with growing electricity demand. Moreover, in times of drought, hydro-dependent countries can find themselves facing serious electricity shortages, as occurred in Zimbabwe and Zambia when there was low water behind the Kariba Dam on the Zambezi River between the two countries.[43] For low-income countries at the mercy of rainfall, coal can look like a way to take control of one's energy destiny. (Climate change may make rainfall even less reliable over time in a number of geographies.) Cambodia, Ethiopia, Malawi, Mozambique, Zambia, and Zimbabwe were all classified as low income by the World Bank as of 2016, and all source the majority of their electricity from hydropower. According to Coalswarm's Global Coal Plant Tracker, all of these countries are eyeing expansions of coal power.[44]

## Will we run out of coal?

With all the countries that continue to rely on coal for their long-term power supply, is there a risk we will run out? The short answer is no. Concerns about running out of fossil fuels have been around for as long as humans have used fossil fuels. "Peak oil" is the best-known concern today, but it is hardly a new one. In 1875, the chief geologist of the state of Ohio, John Strong Newberry, predicted oil would soon run out.[45] In 1909, USGS geologist David Day predicted US oil reserves might last through 1935.[46] In 1973, US State Department official James E. Akins argued that the world's oil reserves were no longer sufficient to meet the world's needs and sounded a particular note of concern about their concentration in the Middle East.[47] As geographer Roger Stern has described, this kind of "oil scarcity ideology" has distorted US foreign policy for many years.

Less well known, perhaps, is the fact that analogous "peak coal" worries have also been around for as long as coal has. As far back as the 1700s, European countries worried that their global dominance would be undercut by the depletion of coal.[48] John Williams laid out these fundamental tenets of mineral scarcity ideology in the context of coal in his 1789 book, *The Natural History of the Mineral Kingdom*.[49] Economist William Jevons, in his 1865 book *The Coal Question*, was not quite as absolute as Williams in his forecast of coal's inevitable scarcity, but he hewed to a broadly peak coal position in arguing that reserves would not grow and technological advancement would only hasten coal's depletion.[50] Some contemporary commentators continue to make peak coal arguments, suggesting that high coal use scenarios can never come to pass because of geological scarcity.

This peak coal argument might be comforting to

environmentalists concerned about climate change, but the model of resource scarcity that underlies it is faulty. Like other fossil fuels, coal is an exhaustible (or non-renewable) resource. Coal originated from organic matter in prehistoric swamps and formed over millions of years, so the amount of coal in the ground will not increase. If one doesn't think too hard about it, this appears to mean we will eventually run out. The idea that there exists some fixed quantity of burnable rock, or burnable liquid, or burnable gas, is intuitive and easy to grasp. It's also wrong. In practice, the quantity of energy-rich material in the earth's crust is far beyond our ability to ever use. What determines when we stop using it is not when we run out, but when the cost of producing a given form of energy exceeds the cost of alternatives, or when alternatives start to provide energy in a more convenient form.

The cheapest, most accessible resources are always extracted first – assuming, of course, that producers have access to them. (Many governments do not allow open access to their resources, so these may not be tapped as quickly, as in the case of oil in Saudi Arabia, for example.) As cheaper resources are depleted, more expensive energy is produced. In the case of coal, the depletion of lower-cost resources manifests as "mine depletion." For example, Indonesia's production has shifted toward lower-rank coals over time as the higher-rank coals are mined out.[51] Both Indonesia and Australia have seen costs rise as coal producers have been forced to mine deeper coal seams located further from coastal loading ports.[52]

However, there is another critical factor that operates alongside resource depletion, and that is technological change. As "easy" reserves of a fossil fuel are depleted, the price of that fossil fuel tends to go up. This creates a strong incentive for energy producers to innovate in developing technologies that drive down the costs of finding and producing the resource. The shale gas revolution in North America was a perfect example of how technological innovation driven by high market prices can expand the available energy supply. It was long known that massive quantities of natural gas were locked in shale layers underground. The problem was that these shales weren't porous enough, so very little gas would actually flow to a well drilled into the shale. In addition, the shale layers were thin, so even if gas could flow a short distance to a conventional, vertical well, it would take so many such wells to extract substantial gas that the process wouldn't be economic. In the 2000s, US natural gas prices were high and rising, and policymakers and analysts anticipated a supply–demand gap that would soon necessitate substantial gas imports. The companies that pioneered the extraction of shale gas saw the high gas prices and realized there were substantial profits to be made from finding cost-effective ways to get the gas out. Through cycle after cycle of experimentation, they discovered that the combination of three technologies – advanced seismic imaging to show where the hydrocarbons were, horizontal drilling to send a wellbore horizontally through the shale layer, and hydraulic fracturing to break open channels in the rock for gas to flow – could allow economic extraction of shale gas. Ongoing innovation since then has continued to reduce cost and make more shale gas deposits economic, turning the US from a declining producer into the world's gas powerhouse.

The same dynamic of technological innovation happens in coal extraction. Easier-to-mine deposits are depleted, but technological innovation can have a countervailing effect, making more resources economic to extract. Innovations in coal extraction technology have kept coal cost-competitive over the decades even as the easiest-to-mine reserves have been depleted. For underground mines, the migration to longwall mining methods was one of the most important cost-reducing innovations. In surface mining, the application of massive excavating and earth-moving equipment like draglines, bucket wheel excavators (as pictured on the cover of this book), and electric and hydraulic shovels has allowed major economies of scale to be achieved. (Chapter 3 describes these shifts in more detail.)

The "peak coal" mindset misunderstands the concept of an energy reserve just as the "peak oil" mindset does. A reserve is the quantity of a fossil fuel that is economic to extract *with current technology at current prices*. By definition, reserves are not fixed. There is no giant stockpile of coal underground that we mine until it is barren, just as there is no giant barrel of oil that we tap until it runs dry. The increase of North American oil and gas reserves due to innovations in seismic imaging, horizontal drilling, and hydraulic fracturing is a striking example of how reserves can go up when prices are high and technological innovation takes place in response. Exploitation of a given resource will continue not until the resource is gone, but until technological innovation can no longer keep such exploitation profitable. As energy economist Morris Adelman memorably put it:

> The total mineral in the earth is an irrelevant non-binding constraint. If expected finding-development costs exceed the expected net revenues, investment dries up, and the industry disappears. Whatever is left in the ground is unknown, probably unknowable, but surely unimportant: a geological fact of no economic interest.
>
> M. A. Adelman (1990), "Mineral depletion, with special reference to petroleum," *Review of Economics and Statistics* 72(1), February 1990.

"Peak coal" will not happen, then, because we run out of coal. It will happen when coal is no longer economically competitive against other forms of energy. This will depend on factors including technological advancements in extracting coal, technological advancements in alternatives to coal, and the degree to which coal's environmental disadvantages are factored into market prices for extracting and using it.

## Critiquing the energy security rationale for coal

Rightly or wrongly, coal is the one energy source most governments – especially growing, energy-constrained ones – seem to believe will always be there for them in ample quantities at an affordable price. This view is usually underpinned by one or more of the following arguments: (1) many countries have significant reserves of coal, (2) a number of countries can reliably export coal to countries with insufficient resources of their own, (3) coal is cheap to extract and relatively cheap to ship, so delivered prices should remain low, and (4) alternatives to coal are likely to remain less energy secure than coal. In the remainder of this chapter, we critique these various arguments.

It is certainly true that many countries that consume coal have a lot of it. China, Russia, Australia, India, and, especially, the United States, sit on massive coal reserves. In the case of China and India, coal reserves dwarf reserves of other energy resources. It seems intuitive that these domestic energy resources would be more trustworthy than imports.

However, the fact that energy comes from domestic sources is far less important for avoiding energy supply disruptions than most people think. India experienced major blackouts in 2012 not because of any coal shortage, but because drought conditions and the resulting agricultural load for irrigation laid bare major problems in the robustness of the electric grid. Japan in 2011 faced its biggest electricity disruption in recent decades not because energy imports to the island nation were cut off, but because of a domestic nuclear accident that might have been avoided with stronger regulatory oversight of plant siting and design. Puerto Rico's power system was devastated in 2017 by the combination of Hurricane Maria, an aging and poorly maintained grid, and an institutional response that was severely wanting; fuel supply per se was not the binding issue.[53] As these examples illustrate, the vast majority of major energy supply disruptions have resulted from the combination of unforeseen events (most typically severe climate events or natural disasters), physical infrastructure vulnerabilities, and institutional and regulatory failures. Hostile actions by foreign actors are a relatively rare cause.

When disruptions with a foreign origin have occurred, as in the Russia–Ukraine natural gas dispute in 2009, countries with resilient markets and infrastructure have been less affected.[54] Even the archetypal example of vulnerability to foreign control over energy, the oil embargo of 1973, would have been a relative non-issue if oil-consuming countries like the United States had not responded with counterproductive economic policies like price controls and rationing.

Moreover, a noteworthy share of coal used around the world is *already* imported, so it's harder to argue in such cases that coal is inherently more secure by virtue of being domestic. India imported 30% of the coal it consumed in 2015, compared with 38% of the natural gas it consumed.[55] Because its coal consumption is so much larger than its gas consumption, India was in fact importing much more coal on an absolute energy basis than it was natural gas. So even though the country's domestic coal resources are much more substantial than its domestic gas resources, depending on coal still means depending on imports.

Barring strong climate change policy on a global level – which seems unlikely in the near future – it is a reasonable assumption that imported coal will remain available at affordable prices. When the IEA laid down its principles on coal in 1979, it was worried about the market power of the OPEC cartel, and one attraction of coal was the fact that it came from a different set of countries, including OECD members like Australia, the United States, and Germany. Rightly or wrongly, no one has ever appeared particularly concerned about the emergence of a "coal cartel." For the moment, there seem to be sufficient exporters to assure supply. Indonesia and Australia are the coal export titans. South Africa has been a traditional swing supplier to either Atlantic or Pacific Basin consumers. Colombia is an important South American supplier. The United States has only tapped a small fraction of its huge and low-cost coal deposits in the Powder River Basin (PRB), and it has the potential to become an important supplier to Asia if Pacific Northwest coal ports are built (*and* if coal prices in Asia are high enough to make exports profitable).

Pacific Northwest coal ports are an interesting test of the proposition that environmental concerns could deter countries from actually exporting coal. When international coal prices were high in 2008 and 2011, proposals were put forward for coal terminals in Oregon or Washington that would enable cheap coal from the Powder River Basin in Wyoming and Montana to be shipped directly to Asia. These plans faced environmental opposition and stalled, but it remains unclear to what extent this outcome was due to environmental objections as opposed to the collapse in international coal prices, which negatively impacted the business model for these ports. (The coal value chain is also robust enough that it might be able to "route around" obstacles like the lack of coal ports in Oregon or Washington, for example through expansion of Canadian coal ports or increased exports from the US Gulf Coast.)

If climate change concerns do start to factor prominently enough into policymaking that they restrict exports in the future, this could at least partially erode the energy security credentials of imported coal. Coal will also become more expensive to use if countries price environmental externalities at higher levels – for example, through a price on carbon that emitters have to pay – or implement other controls on local emissions and/or greenhouse gas emissions. Some environmentalists believe the world will come to recognize that dealing with climate change requires leaving significant coal (and other fossil fuels) in the ground. According to this position, which will be further discussed in Chapter 4, it is an outright financial error to expect to recoup the upfront investment in a coal-fired power plant over a planned lifetime of forty years, as the plant will not be able to operate that long. If investors and energy planners started to factor in a high risk that coal terminals and coal-fired power plants would become "stranded assets" (assets forced to stop operating well before their planned end of life) due to tightening environmental policies, coal would become a less attractive choice for assuring energy security.

The fact that many countries continue to build new coal-fired power plants suggests that planners and investors in these countries do not envision sufficiently high carbon prices (or other environmental policies constraining coal use) anytime soon. That said, there has been some movement on the carbon pricing front. China started regional pilot programs in 2013 and is rolling out the first phase of a national emissions trading scheme targeting the power sector. South Korea implemented an emissions trading scheme in 2015. The carbon prices in China's pilots have been fairly low, generally US \$6/tonne of $CO_2$ and below, but South Korea's carbon prices have been somewhat higher, in the range of \$15–20/tonne.[56] While China is making progress in spreading carbon pricing throughout the country, it is hard to imagine that prices will reach a level that makes natural gas competitive with coal. Neither India nor any other less developed countries in Asia (or elsewhere) have meaningful carbon prices yet.

A final reason coal remains widely favored for energy security is that planners don't yet sufficiently trust the energy security of alternatives. As I discuss in Chapter 5, it is true that alternatives to coal have their challenges at present. At the same time, it is possible that economically viable solutions to these challenges will be developed. For example, wind and solar are only available when there is wind or sun, but improvements in energy storage and expansions of the electricity transmission network could allow this intermittency challenge to be better managed in the future. Nuclear is expensive to build, delay-prone, and widely unpopular, but technology advancements might allow small modular reactors (SMRs) to become a more palatable alternative within several decades.

In most parts of the world, and most notably Asia, natural gas has historically been more expensive than coal. There have also been worries about supply disruptions for gas, especially for countries dependent on pipeline gas. However, supply concerns around gas have been resolved to a significant extent with the deepening of the market for liquefied natural gas (LNG), which nearly twenty countries now export. The price concern might ease if the shale gas revolution ends up spreading from North America to other parts of the world – and especially to China, which has significant shale gas resources. At present, many Asian consumers (including China) receive significant quantities of gas in the form of LNG, which has generally meant a \$4–6/MMBtu transportation premium. If some of this LNG could be replaced by gas produced in the region, it could make natural gas more competitive, just as it is in other countries with substantial domestic production (such as Russia, the United States, the UK, and Argentina, to name a few) or pipeline gas (like most of Europe as well as some Latin American countries). Of course, receiving gas by pipeline does not guarantee low prices if there are few competing sources of gas, and concerns about the supply security of pipeline gas, while often exaggerated, are not entirely unfounded either. (The historical reality is that gas disruptions can be initiated by consumer or transit countries as well as by gas producers, and using gas as a "geopolitical weapon" is rarely in the interest of producing countries, but that doesn't stop pipeline disruptions from occurring from time to time.)[57]

Ultimately, the perception that coal is the most energy secure fuel is unlikely to be dislodged until alternatives to coal are made more competitive by a combination of technological improvement and policy change. In particular, until coal's environmental liabilities are fully factored into its price, it will remain very difficult for other energy sources to compete with coal on cost.

## Conclusion

"Energy security" can be defined in various ways, but it is most usefully thought of as the availability of ample supplies of energy (i.e. enough to avoid constraining energy-using activities) at an affordable price. Coal's first historical role in providing energy security was to free Great Britain from dependence for energy on wood and water, which were both limited in their availability and possible applications. Coal drove a self-reinforcing cycle of industrial development: it fired steam engines, which pumped water from mines to produce more coal, which helped produce iron and later steel, which was used to make steam engines and factories as well as railroads and coal-powered steam locomotives that could transport more coal, and so on. The coal-fueled Industrial Revolution spread to North America and other parts of Europe.

Coal was 50% of the world's energy supply by 1900. Its use continued to trend moderately upward through the first half of the twentieth century even as oil use grew sharply as a fuel for transportation. Developed countries were jolted by two oil shocks in the 1970s, and as a result, they laid out a deliberate policy to limit oil use in electricity generation (where it was more easily replaced than in transportation) and expand coal production and power generation instead, despite long-term climatic risks that were somewhat understood even then. Coal continues to be a major fuel for power generation in many developed countries, while its use has expanded dramatically in developing countries like China and India. Both China and India have pursued policies focused on ensuring energy security for their economies through the use of coal. For the time being, at least, many other developing countries seem intent on following suit.

Even if coal use continues to expand around the world, there is no risk we will run out of coal. One reason is that global coal reserves are substantial, but an even more fundamental reason is that price signals and technological innovation in production will keep us from physically exhausting the supplies of coal, or of any energy resource for that matter. Concerns about "peak coal," in the sense that we will use up the earth's coal supply, have been around since people first started mining the energy-rich rock. Just like concerns about "peak oil," they have always been based on a faulty understanding of economics and technological change.

If coal use is to start declining worldwide, it will be because alternatives have become broadly cheaper and/or better. When this happens is a function both of technological progress in alternatives (as discussed in Chapter 5) and energy and environmental policy. If more countries around the world start to factor in the environmental costs of coal, this will make coal less economically attractive relative to alternatives. Once this occurs, policymakers and planners will no longer view coal as the most "energy secure" fuel. Some environmentalists argue that this day will come sooner than expected, and that countries investing in long-lived coal-fired power plants today are therefore making a financial mistake.

# CHAPTER THREE

# Tensions along the Coal Value Chain

The tension between energy security and economic growth goals on the one hand, and health and environmental concerns on the other, plays out across the coal value chain from mining through transportation through end use. How much coal is used worldwide – and how cleanly it is used – is a function of how the different parts of the value chain are organized and how seamlessly they work together. Environmental groups opposed to coal may seek to disrupt the weakest links in the chain. Politics and policies around coal can also be shaped by the influence of mining, transportation, electric power, and other coal-using industries.

Today's value chain is global, with slightly under 20% of total coal production traded across borders, and the vast majority of that transported by sea.[1] Figure 3.1 shows the most important coal producing and consuming countries, with differences in production and consumption indicating how much a country imports or exports. The ten countries that consumed the most coal on an energy basis in 2017 were, in this order: China, India, the United States, Japan, Russia, South Korea, South Africa, Germany, Indonesia, and Poland.[2] Five of these ten (the United States, Russia, South Africa, Indonesia, and Poland) were net coal exporters. China imported less than 10% of its overall consumption, but China is a large part of the global coal trade in absolute terms, with a strong effect on the price of

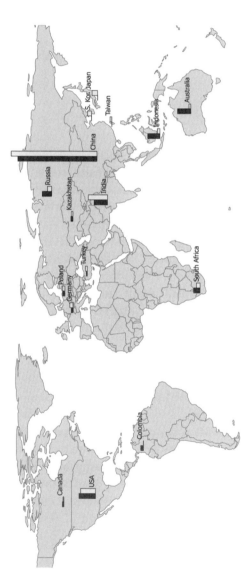

**Figure 3.1** Coal (combined thermal and coking) production (black column) and consumption (white bar) in 2017 for countries among the top twelve in either production or consumption. Units are Mtce (million tonnes coal equivalent) to adjust for the energy content of the coal

*Source:* BP Statistical Review of World Energy 2018

export quality coal in Asia. India imported 30% of its coal, Germany 44%, and Japan and South Korea virtually all.

Japan, South Korea, and Taiwan, with limited energy resources of their own, are highly dependent on coal imports from Australia and Indonesia, which are the biggest coal exporters by far. In Japan, the scaling back of nuclear capacity has made coal particularly crucial. Germany is in a similar situation; with nuclear being phased out because of public disapproval, coal-fired generation has been an important enabler of Germany's renewable energy ambitions. Russia and South Africa both supply significant amounts of coal to Europe and Asia. Colombia and the United States export mainly to Europe, though both have the potential to ship more coal to Asia.

This chapter introduces the different parts of the coal value chain, from mining to transportation to end use, describing: (1) the basic physical details of each activity, (2) health, safety, and environmental concerns associated with each step of the chain, and (3) relevant aspects of industrial structure. The chapter considers characteristic tensions between these parts of the value chain. It explains how these tensions spill over into local, national, and international politics, and what that means for the future of coal.

## Underground mining and its risks

Coal mining is broadly divided into underground mining, where shafts or horizontal passages are dug into the ground to provide access to coal seams, and surface mining, where usually shallower coal deposits are exposed by removing the material above them. Early mining in Europe and North America was underground, both because that's where higher-quality, higher-rank coal was found, and because the machinery to allow cost-effective surface mining did not yet exist.[3] Coal was first mined in England in the 1200s, and it became the country's main fuel by the 1600s.[4] The abundant, easy-to-mine coal resources around Newcastle were particularly important, not least because they could be transported down the River Tyne and shipped by sea to serve London's growing demand.[5]

The earliest underground mining relied on adits, passages driven horizontally into coal seams from exposed outcrops, or bell-pits, simple vertical shafts at the bottom of which miners dug out coal, creating a cross section resembling a bell. The dependence on human and horse power for lifting the coal to the surface and pumping water out of the pits limited the depths from which coal could be extracted. With the advent of coal-powered steam engines in the 1700s, pumping water and moving coal could be mechanized, making it possible to dig much deeper mines.

Early underground mining was especially dangerous, but mine accidents continue to be a serious problem today. Over a thousand miners worldwide die from accidents in a typical year. Underground miners face hazards including structural collapse, poison gases, asphyxiation from lack of breathable air, and explosions. Surface mining is generally safer, though the risks of mine wall collapse and accidents involving vehicles and heavy machinery are still present. The rates of accidents and fatalities from accidents are far higher for coal than for any other energy source, including oil, natural gas, and nuclear power.[6]

The coal mine disasters with the greatest loss of life have involved explosions.[7] The worst disaster in history occurred in 1942, when a methane explosion killed 1,549 in a mine in Northeast China administered by the Japanese Army. But essentially all coal mining regions around the world have at some point experienced mine explosions that killed hundreds of people. And it is not only in emerging economies that mining deaths continue to occur. For example, a 2010 explosion in the Upper Big Branch (UBB) mine in West Virginia killed 29 people.

The typical chain of events leading to a catastrophic explosion is as follows. Methane and other flammable gases that are naturally present in the coal seam reach explosive concentrations and are ignited by a spark or other ignition source. Gas fires or explosions in turn ignite highly explosive coal dust, resulting in blasts that cover huge expanses of an underground mine. Miners not killed in the blasts themselves may succumb to the carbon monoxide left behind by the explosions. It is common for carbon monoxide poisoning to be responsible for the majority of deaths in such accidents.

Technologies for improving safety have advanced over the years to the point where mine disasters are largely preventable if appropriate procedures are followed. Proper ventilation, monitors to detect dangerous gas and dust, and rock dusting (the application of inert minerals to make coal dust less explosive), if correctly implemented, should be able to prevent explosions such as the one that occurred at UBB.[8] And indeed, mine safety performance has gotten better overall through the implementation of these kinds of safety measures.[9] At the same time, there remain significant disparities in mine safety both between and within coal-producing countries. China has historically had the most significant safety problem. Burgherr and Hirschberg (2014) found that China contributed 90% of the accidents and 80% of the fatalities in coal production around the world between 1970 and 2008.[10] (For comparison, China's coal production share increased from about 11% of the global total in 1970 to approximately 45% in 2008.)

Workers in poorly ventilated underground mines also face long-term health risks. Coal workers' pneumoconiosis

(CWP), known colloquially as "black lung" disease, is caused by prolonged exposure to coal dust and kills more miners around the world every year than accidents. The lungs of a miner affected by black lung become laden with coal dust over time, leading to a progressive degradation in lung function. As of 2015, estimates of the number of individuals afflicted with black lung in China varied between 750,000 and 6 million.[11] In the US, over 75,000 coal miners are estimated to have died of black lung since 1968.[12]

Black lung is considered to be largely preventable with proper ventilation and control of coal dust. In the US, the Federal Coal Mine Health and Safety Act of 1969 was successful in reducing both accident rates and the incidence of black lung. The National Institute for Occupational Safety and Health (NIOSH) found that the most deadly form of black lung, progressive massive fibrosis (PMF), dropped to a low of only 0.08% of US miners as of the late 1990s.[13] Since then, however, there has been a marked resurgence in the disease in the US, probably due to some combination of inadequate ventilation and safety practices, increased working hours, and increased coal output. (A correlation with poor ventilation and safety practices is suggested by the fact that autopsies of the victims of the UBB mine explosion showed evidence of black lung in a shocking 71% of cases.)[14] There has also been concern about a reemergence of black lung as a serious health problem in major coal exporter Australia.[15]

## Productivity improvements in mining

Technological advancements in underground mining have boosted productivity. The original underground mining method was a bord and pillar (or room and pillar) scheme, in which coal was removed in a grid pattern, and then the remaining pillars of coal were whittled down until it was deemed structurally unsafe to remove any more coal. A major downside of this approach is that significant amounts of coal, typically over 50%, are left behind. Over time, long-wall mining became more common, significantly boosting productivity (although not all coal seams are suitable for longwall mining). With this mining method, a longwall shearer moves back and forth across a wall to remove coal, and hydraulic supports are put in place to support the roof in the areas where coal has been removed. Where it is feasible, more coal can be recovered with longwall mining, and the method allows more human miners to be replaced with machines.

A shift to more surface mining, enabled by the availability of heavy earth-moving machinery, has also led to major increases in mining productivity. Surface (or open-cut, or opencast) mining techniques remove the material above a coal seam, which is known as the overburden, to get to the coal. Surface mining is only economic for extracting coal that is relatively near the surface, which tends to be lower rank, but for coals near the surface, it can be *very* economic. A modern open-pit mine is essentially a highly mechanized and efficient system for removing and trans-porting dirt and the coal underneath the dirt. It requires significant upfront planning and investment, but little specialized mining knowledge once the mine plan has been developed.

Three main variants of surface mining are: (1) strip mining, in which the overburden and coal underneath are removed in long strips, with the overburden deposited on top of where the previous strip was excavated; (2) open-pit mining, in which the overburden is removed inside a large pit and deposited outside the pit; and (3) mountaintop removal, in which the tops of mountains are blasted off to expose seams of coal at the surface.

Surface mining doesn't expose miners to the dangers of underground operation. It also achieves low capital and operating costs per quantity of coal produced through the use of large and specialized excavating and earth-moving machines. Draglines use huge buckets controlled by wire cables on the end of long booms to remove overburden. Bucket wheel excavators (BWEs), such as the one pictured on the cover of this book, use rotating wheels of buckets to efficiently remove relatively soft overburden and soft coal, which can then be moved away by conveyors. Electric and hydraulic shovels are employed in many surface mines to load coal (and often overburden) into dump trucks for transport away from the mine.

The economies of scale and labor savings of highly automated surface mining have made it extremely cheap. These major cost advantages of surface mining have caused more and more of the world's coal to be produced using this method. In Australia, for example, the share of black coal production from surface mines increased from 2% in 1960 to 67% in 1986.[16] (As a result in significant measure of this shift, output per person more than doubled during this period.) Surface-mined coal in India went from almost nothing in the early 1970s to around 90% of production today.[17] In the United States, surface-mined production was roughly equivalent to underground-mined production in the early 1970s; since then, output from underground mines has stayed more or less constant while surface-mined output, which comes mainly from the Powder River Basin in Wyoming and Montana, has more than doubled.

## The politics of declining coal sector employment

This overall shift from underground to surface mining, coupled with increasing mechanization that has led to productivity improvement in both types of mines, has tended to squeeze out coal jobs in most major coal-producing countries. US coal mining employment peaked at over 800,000 in the 1920s and is currently below 80,000.[18] In China, mine employment declined from a peak of around 6 million to 4.4 million as of 2015,[19] and China's government announced in 2016 that it expected to lay off an additional 1.3 million coal workers to cope with overcapacity in the sector.[20]

Declining coal sector employment reduces the exposure of local communities to problems of mining like mine accidents, black lung, and local environmental impacts, but it also takes away valuable livelihoods. Coal jobs may be dirty and dangerous at times, but they are often comparatively lucrative as well. For example, in West Virginia, the average wage of employees in the coal mining sector in 2011 was more than double the state's average overall wage.[21]

In countries where they exist, state-owned mining enterprises have historically been large and attractive employers. Coal India Limited (CIL) is one such example.[22] CIL is a holding company composed of eight major subsidiaries that together mine close to 85% of India's coal. CIL employs over 300,000 people; at its peak it employed around 650,000.[23] And in practice, the number of direct CIL employees drastically understates the reach of coal into the lives and livelihoods of Indian citizens. Historically, CIL spent massively on a wide variety of public goods and assistance in coal-bearing regions: everything from medical services for family members of employees to development of road, water, and power infrastructure to establishment and operation of schools. Rohit Chandra estimates the total number of people affected by coal company spending in India at 10–15 million[24] (and this still does not consider employment and spending in the railroad and power sectors). Since a major restructuring supported by the World Bank, and a partial privatization starting in 2009,[25] CIL no longer fulfills such a diverse range of tasks, and its operational performance has improved as a result. Still, CIL remains a major locus of economic activity and now provides many local jobs on an outsourced basis, with perhaps 65% or more of CIL's production carried out by private subcontractors.[26]

Because of the importance of mining livelihoods, major reductions in coal mining employment – whether from productivity improvement or other causes – are a problem for politicians, especially where the mining sector is large, as in China and India. Even where coal mining is not as large a contributor to employment and the economy, it can be very significant regionally – and politically influential on the national level. The US only had about 80,000 coal miners as of 2016,[27] not a large share of national employment, but mining remains a significant employer in Appalachian states that are electorally important. And of course, the political problem of declining coal sector employment can be a political opportunity as well. Donald Trump used the promise of bringing back coal to appeal to voters in these regions, implying that coal's declining fortunes were the result of a conspiracy against miners, rather than, more accurately, productivity improvements plus cheap natural gas.

A loose political analogue exists in India. Rohit Chandra points out that the eastern states in India that possess many of the country's coal resources have also been among the more economically depressed states, lagging nationally in income measures. These states have limited renewable energy resources and would not benefit from the national government's ambitious wind and solar plans. On the contrary, renewable expansions over the next two decades could reduce domestic coal-fired power generation, particularly given India's current overcapacity in electricity, and in turn depress coal mining – with negative economic and livelihood impacts on these states. Any perception that the government is putting perceived "elite" concerns about climate change and the environment above local livelihoods could become a political issue in India as it has elsewhere. As Chandra speculates:

> Populist backlash to the perceived injustices of hasty energy transitions have contributed to anti-incumbent electoral swings in both America's and Germany's coal belts. By comparison, India's coal belt is considerably more populous and electorally relevant. These regions may react similarly unless the adverse consequences of [renewable energy] adoption are dealt with.
>
> Rohit Chandra (2018)[28]

Coal is also quite politically influential in Poland, with a substantial number of seats in parliament coming from mining districts. This partly explains why Poland has not kept pace so far with the EU push away from coal and toward renewables, and why the government still envisions an electricity supply mix in 2050 that includes a 50% share for coal.[29]

Political leaders who realistically face up to the downward trajectory of coal mine employment – whether due to increasing productivity or environmental rules or competition from other energy sources – can try to develop retraining programs that equip former miners, or employees of coal-consuming enterprises, for jobs in other industries. It's not an easy task. A big obstacle is the lack of other employment opportunities in coal-mining regions, and the fact that many coal workers are older and may be reluctant or unable to relocate.[30] (Still, innovative approaches may be possible; for example, a Kentucky software development startup called BitSource received a US Department of Labor grant to help train former coal miners to code.)[31]

When China's government announced plans in 2016 to lay off 1.8 million workers in the coal and steel industries (about 15 percent of the workforce), with 1.3 million of them in coal, it said it would set aside RMB 100 million (about $15 billion) to help them find new places in the economy.[32] Because of the size of its coal industry, China's government is extremely sensitive to discontent that could arise from shrinking employment in coal mining as well as coal-using industries. The concern is not unfounded. Even though labor unions are illegal in China, miners have tried to organize to resist the loss of their livelihoods.[33]

## Benefits and harms to local communities

While employment is highly valued, the effects of mining on local communities are complex and multifaceted. In addition to valuable livelihoods, mining can bring significant social ills. Accidents and black lung are two threats to miners that were discussed above. Mining also brings local environmental issues, including threats to the water supply and local bodies of water, deforestation and other alterations to the land to make way for mining, and land subsidence as material is removed underground. Sometimes these environmental issues mean that mine development takes away livelihoods from some even as it provides them to others. This can put local residents on opposite sides of the debate about whether mining should proceed, and how. (In the end, it is common for local communities to have only limited input into decisionmaking, which is a problem in and of itself.)

Water issues can be among the most significant local environmental impacts of mining. Acid rock drainage is one characteristic issue. When mining breaks up rock, it allows water and air to get in and react with sulfide minerals, forming sulfuric acid. The resulting acidic water can dissolve toxic metals naturally present in the rock, producing a stream of acidic, toxic runoff that threatens the safety of water supplies. Coal washeries, which increase the value of coal by removing ash, can pollute waterways. In water-scarce areas, the water needs of mining alone can be seriously disruptive to the watershed. If water use and water pollution are not well regulated by governments, there can be significant harmful impacts on local ecosystems and communities.[34]

The environmental and land use impacts of mining can threaten livelihoods even as mining provides them. In India, coal mining projects that disrupt wetlands have taken away the livelihoods of fishing and agricultural communities.[35] Sometimes new mines involve direct displacement of people living where the mine is going to be.[36] Often the populations being displaced are already marginalized, and mine development further victimizes them and worsens their outcomes.

The historical experience with Cerrejón, a large open-pit mine in Colombia, illustrates the kinds of impacts coal mine development can have on local communities. The area where the mine was established on the La Guajira peninsula was home to both Afro-Colombian and indigenous communities with longstanding ties to the land. The mine project, which was begun in the late 1970s, was originally led by Intercor, a subsidiary of Exxon. In some cases the company offered compensation to displaced families, but its promises of sustained local benefits proved illusory, and the development of Cerrejón ended up rupturing the social fabric of local communities and ending traditional farming livelihoods for many.[37] Air and water pollution were also issues. The mine does provide on the order of 10,000 direct and indirect jobs, and substantial revenues to both private enterprises and the Colombian state, but literacy, health, and economic indicators remain poor for the local communities living near the mine.[38]

In areas where mining has long been a way of life, as in the Appalachian region of the United States, members of local communities are often torn about the environmental issues around mining.[39] Community members may value the mining way of life even as they fear and mourn accidents. They may fear the loss of jobs from mine closures even as they worry about water quality. They may support underground mining even as they oppose mountaintop mining for its impacts on the surroundings.

Ultimately, local communities often find themselves watching helplessly as the battles over coal are fought out in the political arena by forces beyond their control, like large mining and power companies on the one hand and large environmental NGOs on the other.

## Coal transportation

From the early days of coal use to the present, it has been common for transportation to account for a high fraction of the delivered cost of coal. In Britain in the eighteenth century, land transport of coal was estimated to account for about half of the delivered price.[40] In China in the 2000s, during a high-priced period when rail transport was a particular bottleneck, it accounted for 30 to 60% of delivered prices.[41]

The need to move coal more cheaply drove significant improvement in transportation networks during the Industrial Revolution and thereafter. As pointed out by E.A. Wrigley, coal mines are localized, meaning that transport of coal from a mine to a large source of demand will tend to produce heavy, consistent traffic over a single route – and therefore justify investments to upgrade transportation on that route.[42] In this respect, coal was different from the biomass fuel that preceded it. The forests that yielded wood for fuel could stretch over vast tracts of land, so wood harvesting was an "areal" rather than "punctiform" activity, in the words of Wrigley. This meant that moving wood didn't as readily support development of specific transport routes. The imperative to move coal, on the other hand, helped spur the development of canals and, later, rail systems in both Great Britain and the United States.[43] Coal in turn facilitated rail transport by providing steam locomotives with both fuel and a way to make the iron (and later steel) they were made from.

Rail transport is a relatively efficient way of moving coal, but capacity constraints are common, and many routes may be served by a limited number of railroads. Both of these factors can allow railroads to charge high prices. Even when railroads are monopolies charging regulated rates, they may be able to extract extra fees when rail capacity is tight, as occurred in China in the 2000s.[44] Monopolies also may not have strong incentives to expand capacity. State-owned monopoly railroads have at different points been a significant constraint on coal deliveries in India and South Africa.

Even in countries without state rail monopolies, railway regulation can have a crucial influence on delivered coal price, and thus on the economic attractiveness of coal. Several academic studies argue that the decrease in railway transportation costs in the US brought about by railway price deregulation was a more important driver of the shift to lower-sulfur Powder River Basin (PRB) coal than the stringent $SO_2$ regulations of the 1990 Clean Air Act amendments.[45] PRB coal is extracted very cheaply from open-pit mines, but the costs of shipping it long distances by rail had previously limited the degree to which it could compete with Eastern and Midwestern coal in the East, Midwest, and South.

Russia is arguably the country where rail capacity and cost are the greatest constraints on the ability to fully utilize (or export) the available coal. As of the end of 2017, Russia sat on the estimated second-largest reserves of coal, behind only the United States, but its total production was only sixth in the world.[46] One major reason is that a substantial portion of Russia's coal reserves is in remote eastern Siberia, far from ports or large-scale end-use applications. Shipping much more coal by rail than Russia already does could prove prohibitively expensive (and would require high global coal prices to justify). China has a similar problem for its coal resources in Xinjiang, in the far western part of the country. These resources are low cost and high quality, but the expense of expanding rail capacity to ship this coal long distances has led many Chinese analysts to conclude that it would be cheaper to build power plants near the coalfields and build long-distance electricity transmission lines to transport energy as electricity rather than coal.[47] (This is the so-called "coal by wire" approach.)

Shipping coal on waterways has historically been much much cheaper than shipping it by land. The first major coal transportation route – from the coalfields around Newcastle to London – involved moving coal down the River Tyne, along the coast, and then up the River Thames to London. The case of Indonesia vividly illustrates the value of water-borne transport in making coal competitive.[48] In addition to having easy-to-mine coal and being close to major Asian demand centers, Indonesia has historically had the key advantage that many of its coal resources in Kalimantan were close to the Barito and Mahakam rivers and could thus be shipped cheaply by barge. In addition, the benign weather conditions offshore of Kalimantan allow year-round operation of floating trans-shipment facilities to transfer coal from barges to large ocean-going ships. Once coal is loaded on bulk carrier ships, it can be transported across the ocean at relatively low cost. Indonesia's ability to rely on barges and trans-shipment facilities instead of rail-roads and fixed ports let it build out transportation capacity in an inexpensive and modular way, avoiding many of the transportation growing pains of other large coal-producing countries. In fact, the historical importance of Indonesia's waterways for coal transport is being highlighted today by the fact that the Barito and Mahakam rivers are being used at their full capacity for coal transport, the Mahakam faces issues of water level in the dry season that are constraining coal movements, and high-quality coal deposits in North Kalimantan are sitting undeveloped because they aren't close to suitable waterways and need a rail system to be built out.[49]

The world's other gargantuan coal exporter, Australia, has not had the luxury of such easy waterborne transportation. In Australia, rail and port capacity have been periodic constraints since the 1980s, although they are not a major constraint at the current moment.[50] Major infrastructure projects like deepwater ports require significant investment and coordination, and regulatory uncertainty around climate policy and the future of coal can make it even more difficult to plan and build out transportation infrastructure (not to mention coal mines themselves).

When international coal prices were high in 2008 and 2011, there was a strong economic rationale to export cheap coal from the Powder River Basin in the US to Asia. If more coal port capacity had been available in the US Pacific Northwest, significant volumes of coal would likely have been exported. As it was, exports of US steam coal did rise from 1 Mt (million metric tonnes) in 2009 to 10 Mt in 2012, but quantities were limited by port capacity constraints.[51] Starting in 2010, coal producers laid out plans to develop major coal terminals in Washington and Oregon. However, these plans stalled in the face of concerted environmental opposition as well as falling international coal prices that undermined their value proposition. (At the time of writing, international coal prices were trending back upward.)

More generally, coal transportation projects have been a prime target for environmental activists, who have sought to block them at every turn. That said, if the economics of using coal in a particular location are sufficiently attractive, it is likely that producers can find a way to get it there, which is not always the case for other energy alternatives. Even without dedicated ports in Washington or Oregon, some PRB coal still gets to Asia via ports in Canada and the Gulf of Mexico – and there is the possibility that these options could expand further if the value proposition for shipping PRB coal to Asia strenghtens.

When it comes to land transportation, trucks have played a crucial role whenever rail is gridlocked, although trucking coal is expensive. In 2005, 19% of China's coal production was shipped by truck to get around rail constraints.[52] In September 2010, over 10,000 coal trucks became stuck in an epic, 120-km traffic jam in the coal-producing region of Inner Mongolia in northeast China.[53] Road transportation has been an even more crucial link in the coal value chain in India, where limited carrying capacity on the government rail network meant that around 30% of coal moved by truck in 2014–2015.[54]

As much as transportation can be a constraint in the coal value chain, it is still usually less of an issue than it is for coal's most significant competitor in power generation, natural gas. Rail and port constraints can raise costs, but, as described above, there are often workarounds for transporting a bulk solid like coal. For long-distance transportation of natural gas, on the other hand, there are no alternatives to specialized, billion-dollar infrastructure like gas pipelines or the combination of liquefaction plants, liquefied natural gas (LNG) tankers, and regasification facilities on the receiving end.

## Coal power (and pollution)

The greatest share of coal around the world ends up being burned in power plants. According to the International Energy Agency, 66% of primary coal was used to generate electricity and commercial heat in 2015.[55] This share was higher in developed countries, with OECD members using 83% of coal for electricity and commercial heat, and non-OECD countries using 60% for this purpose. The largest non-power-sector application of coal was in steelmaking. Coal also found significant use in generating process heat for various other industrial applications. Several percent of overall coal consumption came from residential use, mainly in China and India.

Almost all coal-fired power plants are equipped with a boiler, steam turbine, generator, a combination of technologies that has been around since the late 1800s. Coal (usually in pulverized powder form) is mixed with hot air and burned in the furnace section of a coal-fired boiler. The heat from the coal's combustion is used to turn water into high-pressure steam. The steam turns the blades of a steam turbine, and the rotary motion is used to turn a generator to produce electricity. The steam is cooled and turned back into water in a condenser, and the cycle continues. The coal-fired power plant can be designed as a combined heat and power plant, with steam bled from the intermediate or low temperature steam cycle of the boiler and delivered as either process steam or heat for industrial or district heating applications.

Traditional "subcritical" power plants boil the water to form steam. Modern "supercritical" and "ultra-supercritical" facilities operate at higher pressures where liquid water turns directly to steam without boiling. This allows these more advanced power plants to achieve higher thermodynamic efficiencies, which translates into less coal use and lower emissions per MWh of electricity generated. Supercritical and ultra-supercritical facilities have higher capital costs than subcritical power plants due to the more sophisticated materials needed to handle their higher pressures and temperatures.

Another type of coal power plant that can theoretically achieve high efficiencies is the integrated coal-gasification combined cycle power plant, or IGCC. In this type of power plant, the coal is gasified and the resulting gas is used to fire a combined cycle gas turbine plant just like in natural gas combined cycle gas turbine (CCGT) power plants. One possible advantage of IGCC plants is that they provide a relatively pure stream of exhaust $CO_2$ that could be captured to reduce emissions to the atmosphere. However, pilot IGCC plants have proven difficult and expensive to operate even as the efficiencies of ultra-supercritical plants have soared, and policy incentives for carbon capture remain relatively weak, so the concept seems to have fallen out of favor of late.

The most fundamental challenge of coal-fired power – and indeed of the entire coal value chain – is environmental impact. Coal combustion is the largest single contributor to global greenhouse gas emissions. Coal produced about 45% of $CO_2$ emissions from fuels in 2013,[56] and $CO_2$ from fuels accounts for about 65% of greenhouse gas emissions from human activity, which suggests coal is responsible for somewhere around 30% of global greenhouse gas emissions from human activity.[57] A more immediately visible environmental problem associated with coal burning is air pollution. Coal burned in power plants, industrial boilers, and, in some regions, for residential heating, releases into the atmosphere substantial quantities of sulfur oxides ($SO_x$), nitrogen oxides ($NO_x$), particulates, and other toxic pollutants including mercury.[58]

The most significant health impacts from coal-related pollution are associated with particles less than 2.5μm across, known as PM2.5. These fine particles are emitted directly from coal burning and also from reactions of $SO_2$ and $NO_x$ in the atmosphere, with secondary PM2.5 from $SO_2$ being particularly significant from a health perspective.[59] The Health Effects Institute estimated that PM2.5 specifically from coal combustion in the power sector, industry, and households led to 366,000 premature deaths in China in 2013 (versus 916,000 deaths overall from PM2.5).[60] Guttikunda and Jawahar estimated that PM2.5 from coal burning led to 80,000 to 115,000 premature deaths in India in 2011–2012.[61] (Note that India generates over four times less total electricity with coal than China.)

In addition, coal burning is second only to small-scale gold mining as a source of anthropogenic (human-caused) mercury pollution.[62] Mercury is converted into highly toxic methylmercury in aquatic environments, and it accumulates in fish people eat. Consumption of methylmercury can lead to birth defects and developmental problems, especially in young children.

Coal-fired power plants also cause other environmental issues in the surrounding area. The waste products from burning coal, known collectively as coal ash, must be disposed of properly to avoid negative environmental and health impacts. In countries including Japan, and to a lesser extent Indonesia and the Philippines, ash storage and disposal has become a serious environmental and land use problem.[63] Coal-fired power plants are also heavy users of water for cooling, which can lead to severe water stresses in water-scarce regions. (Water is also used in mining and washing coal.) Production and consumption of coal in northern China has contributed to serious water shortages in that region.[64]

$SO_x$, $NO_x$, particulates, and other toxic emissions from burning coal can be reduced to a large extent with emissions control technologies. Flue gas desulfurization (FGD) removes $SO_x$. Selective catalytic reduction (SCR) and selective non-catalytic reduction (SNCR) remove $NO_x$. Electrostatic precipitator (ESP) and/or fabric filter (FF) technologies remove directly emitted particulates. FGD, ESP, and FF technologies also capture significant mercury.[65] The challenge is that all of these control technologies add cost. One sample analysis suggested that retrofitting a power plant in India with flue-gas desulfurization could add at least 9% to its levelized cost of energy.[66] Because of these kinds of added costs, emissions controls may not be mandated by regulations, or even if they are, the regulations may not be well enforced. In developing country environments, there is often little appetite for spending more on emissions controls while meeting basic energy needs still seems like the more immediate concern. Even where there is the desire to control emissions, government monitoring and enforcement capability may not be up to the task.

Controlling emissions from large central station power plants is easier than controlling emissions from industrial and other smaller sources. Power plants are typically large, few in number, and operated by power companies (perhaps government-owned ones) over which the government can more readily exert control. Industrial boilers are usually smaller, more numerous, and more difficult to control. The case of China illustrates the difficulty. While about 60% of China's coal consumption occurs in the power sector,[67] a significantly smaller share – closer to one-quarter – of its ambient PM2.5 concentrations are attributable to coal-fired power plants.[68] This reflects the significantly higher efficiencies and better emissions controls of China's large power plants relative to industrial boilers that burn coal for process heat. (A smaller but not-insubstantial portion of China's PM2.5 problem comes from residential burning of coal for heating and cooking, which is especially common in major coal-producing provinces such as Shanxi and Inner Mongolia.)

In a fast-growing economy, there can be significant tension between the desire to quickly and cheaply build out coal-powered end uses and the desire to maintain good air quality. The next section discusses ways in which the coal value chain can tend to resist change, including when it comes to implementation of tighter environmental rules.

## The coal value chain fights back

Both coal producers and coal consumers may fight back against efforts to regulate them on environmental or safety grounds. For example, China's central government has faced resistance from local authorities to its efforts to stamp out small, unauthorized mines. The efficiency of these small mines is lower than that of the large, modern operations, and their safety performance is significantly worse. In 2009, for example, town and village enterprise (TVE) coal mines were responsible for around one third of Chinese coal production but two thirds of all deaths from coal mine accidents.[69] (China's overall fatality rate per tonne of coal produced has decreased by about a factor of thirty since 1950, but as of 2013 there were still over a thousand mining deaths from accidents in a typical year.)[70]

However, these small mines have proven stubbornly difficult to stamp out. One reason is that small mines provide crucial swing capacity in times of tight supply. After all, the central government originally encouraged the development of TVE mines in the 1980s because production from SOE mines could not meet demand. Even more importantly, though, the majority of China's coal production is controlled at the local level, and these small operations contribute significantly to local economies while providing revenue to local governments. What has sometimes happened in the past when the central government has tried to close these mines is that they keep producing but stop reporting their output, with the implicit support of local governments. As detailed by China energy expert Kevin Jianjun Tu, these "grey markets" for coal have led at times to systematic underreporting of China's coal production, which was especially pronounced following the central government's campaign to shut down small mines in the late 1990s.[71]

Small, informal, and often illegal mines are not unique to China. Kuntala Lahiri-Dutt performed field surveys in eastern India suggesting that illegal collieries numbered in the thousands and collectively produced millions of tonnes of coal.[72] Many of these mines are dangerous, and they exploit poor, marginalized people as their labor force. On the other hand, these illegal mines do provide livelihoods for these miners, and they are able to serve coal demand free from the strictures of Coal India Limited and formal government control of the sector. As in the case of China, local governments may tolerate these mines.

It is not only in their efforts to control mining that central governments have faced pushback; they have also struggled at times to put the brakes on coal-using industries as part of efforts to reduce pollution and curb overcapacity. In China, local officials in the province of Hebei were reluctant to enforce a central government order to shut down local steel mills because of the employment and other economic benefits the mills provided, especially as China's economy slowed overall.[73] Just as in the case of TVE coal mines, steel producers have sometimes stopped reporting their output rather than submitting to the shutdown order.[74]

In another sector, China's largest aluminum producer, China Weiqiao Group, has at times seemed able to sidestep government restrictions on both aluminum production capacity and use of coal power, which it generates through a subsidiary for its own use in the energy-intensive process of aluminum smelting.[75] China Weiqiao is a major employer in its home province of Shandong, and close relationships with local governments have helped it prosper over the years.

Resistance by coal mining and coal consuming interests to environmental rules that adversely affect coal is hardly unique to China. In Germany, the powerful coal lobby successfully turned back a levy in 2015 that would have targeted emissions from power plants fired with highly polluting lignite, of which Germany has substantial reserves.[76] The pro-coal group argued that the levy could have put 100,000 German jobs at risk. Also in 2015, miners and their trade unions in Poland threatened to bring down the government over a law they saw as threatening mines and mining jobs.[77] In response, the government committed to keeping the mines open. In the United States, where competition in the marketplace from cheap natural gas has hurt the domestic coal industry,[78] coal interests have pushed hard for government subsidies.[79] In response, the Trump administration proposed various rules that would compensate coal (and nuclear) power plants for their supposedly special energy security value in the grid, even though there was no rigorous analysis suggesting they actually provide such value.[80]

In countries where the financial sector has leant heavily to coal producing or coal consuming companies, banks may lobby against government actions that could reduce coal's role. For example, when China's government pushed hard to trim overcapacity in coal and steel production, some commentators argued against moving too fast against industries that were RMB 8 trillion ($1.2 trillion) in debt as of 2016 – with about one-third of this debt held by Chinese banks.[81] Precipitous action, these commentators argued, risked further endangering already-tenuous bank balance sheets, with local banks likely to suffer the worst impacts. Low coal prices (which have since recovered significantly) made the problem look especially acute at that time. More broadly, a number of problems in China's financial sector can be traced back to the way the government used state-owned enterprises to achieve policy goals while directing state-owned banks to support them in doing so, including by supplying credit to support the takeover by state-owned enterprises of small, unregulated mining operations.

In India, the larger risk to the state-owned banking sector could come from its exposure to coal-fired power plants. As noted by Rohit Chandra, international investors have shied away from participation in the Indian power sector ever since Enron's Dabhol power project turned sour starting in the mid-1990s, which has left Indian state-owned banks as the major source of credit for coal-fired power plants in the country. (Dabhol was an ambitious naphtha- and natural-gas-fired power project that became a financial debacle for reasons including political opposition in India, non-payment by Maharashtra's State Electricity Board, questionable project design and community engagement by US company Enron, and Enron's scandal and bankruptcy.) If coal plant operations were to be ramped down too quickly, it could possibly be detrimental to the health of India's state-owned banking sector.[82]

Even in countries with less direct government involvement in markets, there are various possible ways the coal value chain could resist change. To take one example, economist Louis Preonas has shown how the effect of carbon pricing on coal use in the United States could be blunted by the structure of rail markets.[83] Railroads in the US sometimes have local market power that contributes to their profit margins from shipping coal. For example, when a coal-fired power plant is served by only a single railroad, the railroad is able to set rates so coal is just cheap enough that the plant can still make money by running, but no cheaper. The railroad knows there is no competing coal shipper that can undercut it on price. If a carbon price is put in place, Preonas points out, railroads in this position are likely to accept a reduction in their profit margins, reducing their rail rates just enough to compensate for the carbon price and ensure that their customers won't stop operating their coal plants. This imperfectly competitive rail market means that the reduction in coal use from establishing a carbon price in the US might not be as large as it otherwise would be. Similar dynamics could occur in other countries.

The fact that the coal value chain is global also has policy ramifications. Countries that put a substantial price on carbon or limit coal use through other means will reduce demand for coal inside their borders. However, since coal is traded on a global market, this reduction in aggregate demand will also tend to reduce the price of coal in other countries, which could cause them to use more. Overall coal use might still go down, but the global character of the coal value chain could mean it wouldn't go down as much as one would otherwise expect.

## The coal–power conflict

One of the most characteristic conflicts in the coal value chain is between the coal sector and the power sector. In many countries, the power sector is tightly regulated and subject to price controls while the coal sector operates on a more market basis. This can result in a situation where the regulated prices power companies charge for electricity don't cover the costs of procuring market-priced coal. On top of this, the rail system in between the coal and power sectors may become a constraint and price adder of its own.

In China, the problem of manifold coal companies trying to come to terms on price and quantity with the big state-owned power companies is so salient that "coal-power conflict" (*mei dian ding niu*) and "market coal versus planned electricity" (*shichang mei miandui jihua dian*) are established terms. The coal-power conflict became especially severe when soaring coal prices in 2008 led to big losses for state-owned generators, and talks broke down at the 2009 Coal Conference that was supposed to facilitate contracts between coal and power producers. Coal-fired power plants kept generating, so bilateral contracts were presumably negotiated on the side, but this problem in the coal value chain led to changes in behavior and policy. Power producers started importing more coal to get a better price,[84] and the central government pushed harder on vertical integration as a possible solution to these value chain tensions.[85] The coal-power conflict in China has also been a proxy conflict between the central government, which controls the power sector, and local governments, which control the majority of mining.

In India, power producers have traditionally obtained coal at artificially low prices by being granted a formal "linkage" to a mine.[86] This is a bureaucratic, centrally planned process, and many power producers struggle to get as much below-market-priced coal as they would like. (By trying to force suppliers to deliver a quantity of a certain product at a price below that at which they would naturally want to supply that quantity, artificial price caps like this inevitably cause shortages.) Power producers have blamed state-owned Coal India Limited for production shortfalls and a failure to deliver contracted quantities of artificially cheap coal, which has forced these power producers to procure market-priced coal through an "e-auction" mechanism or to import significant quantities of coal at international prices.[87] Arguably, though, the deeper root problem is the tenuous financial model of most of India's state-level electricity distributors. Electricity tariffs in most Indian states are not sufficient to recover the costs of generation when coal is procured at market rates. Until this and other problems in India's electricity sector are fixed, including electricity theft and non-payment, the country will continue to face this variety of "coal-power conflict." If these downstream problems in the coal value chain were fixed – not to mention the serious upstream challenges of acquiring land for new coal mines[88] – it is possible that India would consume even more coal than it already does. (On the other hand, the dysfunctions in India's electricity sector can also impede procurement of competing fuels like natural gas.)

One of India's attempted solutions to the dysfunctions of its coal value chain has been some limited vertical integration in the form of "captive mining." The idea was to let private enterprises that consume coal – for example, power and steel companies – expand upstream to mine and transport their own coal, which could also have the benefit of sidestepping the constraints of the state-owned rail monopoly. (CIL and the state-owned rail monopoly, Indian Railways, have been at loggerheads for years, with negative effects on coal deliveries and the economy, especially in the late 1970s and early 1980s.)[89] Nimble and politically connected private firms have had some success in captive mining. Still, they have never had the political heft of a state-owned enterprise (SOE) like Coal India Limited that directly employs hundreds of thousands of Indians and indirectly employs many more.

China has also tried vertical integration as a way to mitigate value chain problems, most notably by letting its big central-government-owned SOE in coal, Shenhua, expand downstream into transportation and power generation. Vertical integration of power companies back upstream into coal mining and rail transportation to give them "captive" coal and rail has also been tried by China's big state-owned power corporations, which have wanted to make sure coal and rail do not constrain their core power businesses.[90] In the case of Shenhua, at least, vertical integration appears to have been successful so far, with the company operating along the entire coal value chain. Its activities include mining, coal transportation, coal port operation, coal-fired power generation, and chemical conversion of coal (such as production of liquid fuels). China's government sought to take Shenhua's vertical integration to the next level in August 2017 by approving a mega-merger between Shenhua and Guodian, one of China's "Big 5" power producers that also had some appreciable coal production.

The cases of China and India highlight a fundamental tension in governance of the coal value chain between the desire to tightly control prices and outcomes on the one hand and the need to actually match supply to demand on the other. Both governments have a fundamental inclination toward direct involvement in the coal value chain, given that it is so important to national economic development. That's why India has subsumed most coal mining under Coal India Limited. That's why China's coal sector used to be dominated by central-government-owned SOEs,[91] and it's why the government created Shenhua in 1995 as a major state-owned coal producer. (Shenhua is not so different from Coal India Limited in the absolute tonnage of coal it produces, but Shenhua's output is closer to 10% of China's overall production, versus CIL's 85% share in India.)[92] The difficulty is that central planning and government ownership are frequently ineffective at ensuring coal production meets demand. That's why India has experimented with captive mining and market pricing for some portion of domestic coal. It's why China began to liberalize coal prices and let private enterprises play a larger role in the sector starting in the 1980s, when flagging coal output became a drag on the economy.[93] The imperative of boosting production led to the creation of the town and village enterprise (TVE) mines, which absorbed rural labor and helped significantly increase national coal output.[94] Starting in the late 1990s, China also transferred ownership of many financially troubled mines from the central government to local governments, with the end result that the central government today controls only a minority of production, mainly through Shenhua and China Coal.[95]

When the need to maximize output recedes as a priority relative to other goals such as safety or the environment, governments may try to reassert control, though not always with complete success. For example, TVE mines have fallen out of favor with China's central government in recent years due in part to their poorer safety record, and the government has tried to shut them down. However, local governments that benefit from TVE mining have often resisted such efforts, as discussed above. India's government has tried to impose tighter environmental regulations on power plants, but the power sector has resisted.

In major coal exporting countries like Indonesia, Australia, and South Africa the coal-power conflict can manifest as the tension between exporting coal, possibly for higher prices, and selling to power producers at home. One typical approach, as exemplified by South Africa, is "export the best and burn the rest" – basically, export the highest quality coal, which can fetch the best prices on the international market, and tailor domestic power plants to use the lower quality coal left over.[96] It's important for policymakers to bear in mind that exports versus domestic use is not a zero sum game over the long term. The prospect of earnings from exports – for example to Japan starting in the 1970s – played a major role in driving the development of the coal sectors of Indonesia, Australia, and South Africa, which in turn made large amounts of coal available for domestic use in these countries. That said, when coal markets are tight, and especially when there are coal production shortfalls and transportation constraints in a coal-producing country, there tends to be political pressure to keep more coal at home. If domestic and export coal prices were equal, of course, the coal producer would be indifferent as to whether it sold the coal at home or for export; the catch is that big domestic consumers like power companies typically expect to get domestic coal at a lower price. Indonesia has a Domestic Market Obligation (DMO) intended to make sure there is enough domestic coal available to support the country's expansion of coal-fired power generation.[97] Needless to say, policies like DMOs are not popular among coal producers, who would always like to sell their product at the highest possible price, or among international customers, who want to be sure their contracts for coal supply will be honored.[98]

## Conclusion

The relative robustness of coal's value chain can be one of the fuel's attractions. Coal can be mined in labor-intensive ways that require relatively little upfront investment, or in modern surface mines with high upfront investment but low cost overall. Coal is most efficiently transported over land by rail, but trucks work too if rail is constrained, and water transport, where feasible, is usually cheapest overall. Modern ultra-supercritical power plants are highly capital intensive, but coal can be burned in a cheap and dirty way in industrial boilers or even home furnaces. As we will discuss in Chapter 5, the relative ease of building out a value chain for coal is in contrast to coal's most direct competitor, natural gas, which involves expensive, specialized transportation infrastructure that requires complex coordination between investors, gas field developers, and prospective end users.

At the same time, there are frictions along the coal value chain that can increase cost and negatively affect coal consumption. Railroads are often a constraint or cost adder, especially in cases where rail capacity and competition are limited. Tensions between the coal and power sectors are also common. Many important power sectors around the world are dominated by state-owned monopolies that are not allowed to charge a market price for electricity – and in turn struggle to pay market prices for coal. China and India have both experienced their own versions of this "power-coal conflict," which in its most serious form can constrain power production and serve as a brake on the economy.

Even where the coal value chain does not work entirely seamlessly, it can have a built-in inertia that discourages shifts away from coal. The local economic benefits provided by coal may encourage local governments to resist central government efforts to moderate coal production and use on environmental grounds. In China, for example, huge aluminum and steel producers have sometimes kept operating – and burning huge amounts of coal in dirty and inefficient ways – even as the central government has tried to crack down on pollution and overcapacity. Local state-owned banks in China are heavily exposed to coal and steel. State-owned banks in India are heavily exposed to coal-fired power generation. These kinds of financial sector exposures to coal can discourage national governments from shifting away from coal too rapidly. More generally, the jobs coal provides, especially in politically important regions, may discourage politicians from opposing coal.

In the winter of 2018, China got an unwelcome reminder that rapidly replacing the coal value chain is not so easy. The central government tried to ban coal for heating in northern cities in favor of natural gas, with the intention of improving air quality around Beijing. But gas connections lagged, and demand for gas soared (along with LNG prices), and the plan had to be scuttled – for that winter at least.[99] Still, such efforts show how stronger environmental policy has the potential to limit coal use, add cost across the coal value chain, and make other energy sources more competitive against coal, as we will examine in the next chapter.

CHAPTER FOUR

# Environmental Politics and Policymaking

## Incorporating environmental externalities

A major reason the world still uses so much coal – in addition to coal's advantages of production cost, wide geographical distribution, and value chain robustness – is that few governments account for the full social costs of energy. Most rich countries have reasonably stringent and well-enforced rules on emissions of local pollutants like $SO_x$, $NO_x$, and particulates, but many developed countries have weaker regulatory capability and have focused first and foremost on meeting the energy needs of their rapidly growing economies. One result, as discussed in the previous chapter, has been major health problems from respiratory disease.

Another social cost of energy production and use is its contribution to climate change, which is particularly relevant in the case of coal because of its high $CO_2$ emissions (typically 0.9–1.0 tonnes of $CO_2$ per MWh of electricity generated in a reasonably efficient power plant). The "social cost of carbon" (SCC) is a measurement of the negative economic impact of one tonne of $CO_2$ emitted into the atmosphere. To put one tonne of $CO_2$ into context, the average passenger vehicle in the United States emits five tonnes of $CO_2$ in a year,[1] and five tonnes of $CO_2$ is also about what is emitted in a year to generate the electricity to power an average US home.[2]

The calculated value of the social cost of carbon is highly dependent on input assumptions – for example, the discount rate used to calculate the present value of future economic impacts – and it is also difficult to estimate due to the uncertainty in climate change impacts. Depending on the assumptions used, the value of the SCC can range from less than $20 to hundreds of dollars or more.[3] As of mid-2016, the US government estimated the 2015 value of SCC at $36/tonne of $CO_2$ (in 2007 dollars), while acknowledging that this did not take into account all impacts of climate change.[4]

The harms of the pollution and greenhouse gas emissions that come from producing and using coal (and other forms of energy) are what economists call negative externalities – costs to society that accrue from private economic transactions but are not paid for by the parties to those transactions. Unless environmental regulations specifically require it, neither the operator of a coal-fired power plant nor the consumer buying its electricity have to pay the social cost associated with the coal plant's contribution to smog or climate change. Incorporating externalities into these transactions in the form of an emissions price would create incentives for coal-fired plants to install emissions control technologies – and also allow inherently cleaner energy sources to compete with coal more effectively. Alternatively, governments might choose to address environmental harms through "command and control" regulations. These could, for example, require specific emissions control technologies, or mandate that a certain share of energy come from renewable or other zero-carbon sources, or even ban coal use altogether. Command and control regulations are sometimes easier for governments to implement (and explain to their constituents) than emissions pricing, but they increase the cost of achieving environmental goals by limiting the options available to meet them.

Because of coal's high carbon footprint, putting a price on carbon could have an important impact on how much coal is used. There are two main types of carbon pricing: a tax on carbon, where emitters are directly charged per tonne of $CO_2$ they release into the atmosphere, and a cap-and-trade system (also known as a carbon market or emissions trading system). In a cap-and-trade system, a certain number of emissions "allowances" are made available, where each allowance permits its holder to emit one tonne of $CO_2$ without penalty. These allowances are tradable, so a market participant that can reduce emissions more cheaply than the market price of the allowance can sell it to another market participant for whom emissions reductions would be more expensive. These days, allowances are commonly allocated to market participants through auctions, though governments sometimes distribute a certain quantity of allowances for free (which is essentially giving away free money) as a way to curry support for the program.

A detailed discussion of the differences between a carbon tax and a cap-and-trade system is beyond the scope of this book, but the most obvious difference is that the carbon tax sets a fixed price for carbon, with emissions allowed to fluctuate, whereas the cap-and-trade system sets a fixed quantity of emissions, or cap, with carbon price allowed to fluctuate. (In practice, there are reasons why all carbon caps are less firm than they appear, and cap-and-trade systems work best if they are designed with a floor price and a ceiling price for carbon). If properly designed and implemented, both forms of carbon pricing can incentivize the desired reductions in greenhouse gas emissions. In addition, they both raise revenue for governments (assuming, in the cap-and-trade case, that allowances are allocated by means of auctions).

This revenue can be used either to expand the government budget and fund additional programs or to reduce economically inefficient and unpopular taxes like income taxes, with no net change in government revenue. This latter approach is the "revenue-neutral" carbon tax, which seems like it should be more popular than it has thus far proven.

For all the advantages of carbon pricing, only about 20% of the world's greenhouse gas emissions are currently covered by carbon pricing regimes, and no large, broad-based carbon pricing programs have a carbon price as high as most estimates for the social cost of carbon. To provide a few examples, the carbon price in South Korea's emissions trading system was reasonably significant at the time of writing (around \$20/tonne of $CO_2$) while the level of Japan's carbon tax (around \$3/tonne of $CO_2$) was not; the United Kingdom had in place an appreciable carbon price (its carbon price "floor," at around \$24/tonne of $CO_2$), while the carbon price in the EU Emissions Trading Scheme had recovered significantly, to around \$16/tonne of $CO_2$; and the United States had no national carbon price, but California's emissions were covered by a state-level cap-and-trade system with a carbon price of around \$15/tonne of $CO_2$. Among developing countries, China had taken the most significant action, with regional carbon trading pilots in place (carbon prices between \$1 and \$10/tonne of $CO_2$) and a national program in the works. (The World Bank provides valuable ongoing tracking of the status of carbon pricing around the world.)[5]

## Drivers of environmental policy

What explains the variation in environmental policy across countries? In the 1990s, economists observed that environmental quality tended to be better in places with high per capita income.[6] A pattern whereby pollution grows worse as countries start to develop and then decreases again once they pass a certain threshold of economic development, in an inverted-U pattern, became known as the "environmental Kuznets curve." The literature on environmental Kuznets curves is long and contentious, and researchers have struggled to prove a causal relationship between income – or other variables – and environmental quality. However, the broad fact remains that richer countries have generally done more in the area of environmental regulation, especially when it comes to limiting local pollution.

In a 2006 paper, economist Charles Kolstad laid out a conceptual model of the environmental Kuznets curve that can serve as a helpful framework for considering the future of environmental regulation – and its effect on coal – around the world.[7] Kolstad considers the supply and demand for reductions in the emissions of a given pollutant. At low levels of economic development, there is low demand (willingness to pay) for pollution reduction because other concerns like income and employment are more pressing. As heavy-emitting industry expands with growing income and development, reducing pollution becomes more expensive – i.e. the "supply curve" for emissions reductions shifts up – and emissions go up. At high levels of economic development, people's basic needs are satisfied and the demand for pollution reductions goes up. At the same time, structural shifts in the economy away from heavy manufacturing and toward services may shift the emissions reduction supply curve down. (It's also possible that shifts away from manufacturing could result in some emissions being "exported" to other countries that have lower income and manufacturing costs.) Together, these demand and supply effects combine to reduce pollution.

Other factors can come into play too. More developed economies may have greater institutional capacity to enforce environmental regulations. Improvements in pollution control technologies or the development of less-polluting alternatives could help shift emissions lower in all countries.

This conceptual framework provides insights into what we might expect when it comes to environmental regulation of coal and other polluting energy sources in different countries. First, public opinion matters. It creates the demand for pollution reductions that politicians eventually feel obliged to heed for their own political survival. We expect that public pressure to improve environmental quality will increase when people have jobs and when their basic needs are met, but the amount of public pressure may vary even between countries with similar levels of economic attainment.

Second, national and subnational institutions shape how public opinion is translated into environmental action. One might expect in general that more democratic political systems would be more responsive to public desires for clean air, but this is not necessarily the case. China is not a democracy, but central government officials are nonetheless acutely aware that the government's popular legitimacy depends on being able to deliver both economic growth and, increasingly, a high quality of life. This includes dealing with the country's serious air pollution problem, and China's authoritarian political system can in some respects be an advantage when it comes to implementing top-down environmental policies like $SO_2$ controls or carbon pricing. (On the other hand, as we discussed in Chapter 3, it has also enabled the implementation of centrally planned policies that have distorted China's economy in problematic ways, including when it comes to the coal value chain.) Whatever a country's political system, the strength of its regulatory institutions is also critical in determining how effectively the intention of government officials to improve environmental quality can be translated into actual results.

Third, technological improvements that reduce the cost of emissions reduction are a crucial step toward dealing with pollution and climate change in all countries, irrespective of their levels of development. Government support is needed for research and development, especially for pathbreaking energy and emissions abatement technologies. Research and development activities can have what are known as positive externalities – social benefits that are not fully captured in private transactions. This can cause private firms to underinvest in research and development in the absence of additional incentives.

Fourth, the global nature of the climate change problem means that we can't count on the mechanisms behind the "environmental Kuznets curve" to drive reductions in greenhouse gas emissions as strongly as they might for local pollutant emissions. As Kolstad explained:

> [T]he big difference is in the connection between individual willingnesses to pay for reduction and regulations to implement that demand. This link is much weaker [for greenhouse gases] than for more localized pollutants and results in a net demand for reductions that is very diluted. As a global pollutant, there is a very imperfect connection between regulatory actions in a country and benefits to the citizens of the country. Thus even in a fully functioning democracy, there is a weak incentive to translate demand for lower global greenhouse emissions into regulations on domestic industry.
>
> Charles Kolstad (2006), "Interpreting estimated environmental Kuznets curves for greenhouse gases," *Journal of Environment and Development* 15(1).

The key problem, in other words, is that emissions reductions are driven in part by the public's willingness to pay for them, and people aren't willing to pay as much for greenhouse gas emissions reductions because these don't affect them as directly (the emissions from their state or country are only a fraction of the global problem) or immediately (time horizons for the worst climate impacts can be decades or more) as local pollution.

One important implication of the above is that local pollution is likely to be a more compelling driver of change than climate concern, especially in developing countries. Dealing with local pollution may result in co-benefits for the climate, as when coal is substituted by cleaner energy sources. However, it doesn't always. Adding emissions controls to coal power plants and moving coal plants away from population centers are two steps that have helped China reduce health risks for its citizens without reducing China's contribution to global greenhouse gas emissions.

The remainder of this chapter explores the ways in which the above dynamics make it difficult to fully incorporate the environmental costs of coal into economic decisions. It specifically considers the cases of China and India and what they say about the process of translating public concern about the environment into actual environmental enforcement. Finally, the chapter examines the possible impact of environmental advocacy organizations on the trajectory of environmental regulation and the future of coal.

## Public support for environmental protection

Stringent environmental regulations will not be enacted anywhere without significant public support. Air pollution causes obvious, immediate degradation in the quality of life of those who experience it and is therefore more likely than climate change to become a source of widespread popular discontent. A Pew Research Center survey in 2015 showed air pollution ranking second among fifteen concerns of respondents in China, behind only corrupt officials.[8] Pollution is more likely to be a top issue when citizens feel generally safe and prosperous. In a different Pew survey in the same year, pollution was also judged "a very big problem" by a significant majority of respondents in India, but it ranked behind crime, lack of employment opportunities, rising prices, and poor-quality schools.[9] In the China survey, by contrast, these other four concerns all ranked behind air pollution, possibly a testament to China's success in providing security, employment and economic welfare, and decent educational opportunities. At the same time, worsening air pollution in India may be causing this issue to grow in perceived importance, as the share of respondents identifying it as a major problem rose 22 percentage points between Pew surveys in 2014 and 2015.[10]

When it comes to climate change, broad majorities in forty countries surveyed by the Pew Research Center in 2015 responded that climate change was a serious problem.[11] Majorities in all but one country (Pakistan) said that climate change is either harming people already or will be in the next few years. At the same time, there were significant partisan divisions around the issue. The United States was the poster child for political polarization of climate change, with 68% of Democrats classifying climate change as a "very serious problem" versus only 20% of Republicans.[12] (82% of Democrats supported limiting greenhouse gas emissions, versus 50% of Republicans.) However, partisan divides were evident in other countries too. In Australia, for example, 72% of Greens supported climate action, compared with 65% of Labor Party members and 31% of Liberals.

Australia highlights a specific danger when it comes to climate policy, which is that measures pushed into law with too narrow a base of political support risk being thrown out when the government changes. Under pressure from Greens to deliver on climate policy, Australia's Labor Party Prime Minister Julia Gillard shepherded into law, on the narrowest of margins, a carbon tax that started in 2012 at a level of AUD$23/tonne of $CO_2$.[13] The unpopularity of the carbon tax, especially among coal and other industry interests, helped precipitate the fall of Prime Minister Gillard, and subsequently the fall of the Labor-led government. In 2014, new prime minister Tony Abbott, from the Liberal Party, scrapped the carbon tax. Other countries – and democracies especially – are vulnerable to this same kind of climate policy seesaw. In the United States, for example, the Trump administration has worked to roll back federal climate change efforts (and other environmental rules) initiated under the Obama administration.

Australia and the United States illustrate another feature of public opinion around climate, which is that, on average, people in countries with high per capita greenhouse gas emissions tend to report being less concerned about climate change, whereas people in countries with lower per capita emissions tend to report being more concerned. Both Australia and the United States have high, and similar, $CO_2$ emissions per capita. Both countries are on the low end when it comes to public concern about climate change as measured by the Pew study.[14] It is not clear whether lower public concern around climate change *leads* to higher emissions, or whether people whose countries emit more rationalize these emissions as relatively less important, or whether some other dynamic is at play.

Even when climate change is accepted as real and serious by a majority of people – and this is the case even in the United States, Australia, the UK, Poland, and Israel, which ranked lowest in Pew's classification of "climate change concern" – climate may not be high enough on people's list of concerns to drive voting patterns. If climate-concerned voters still care more about jobs or other issues, the political process may not effectively translate their climate concern into climate action. The struggles to implement economically sound carbon pricing around the world are symptomatic of the fact that, even in the environmental space, fighting climate change per se doesn't inspire as much passion as more tangible causes. People may hate nuclear power (as in Germany and many other countries), or love wind and solar (as is the case everywhere), or hate proposed cross-border oil pipelines (as in the United States), but environmental economists seem to be the only ones who love carbon pricing with a passion.

## Institutional capacity and environmental regulation: The cases of China and India

Governments vary in their administrative capacity to tackle environmental problems. Even if pollution is perceived as a pressing problem by the public, and even if there exists the political will to do something, institutional and technical obstacles can prevent the problem from being effectively addressed. China and India provide an instructive comparison. Both countries have severe air pollution problems, with coal a major contributor. As measured by PM2.5 concentrations, ten of the world's top twenty most polluted cities in 2016 were in India, and four were in China.[15] Both countries are trying to address their respective pollution problems, but China is farther along in the process of developing regulatory capability.

Yuan Xu, an expert on air pollution control in China, has documented the country's massive installation of flue gas desulfurization (FGD) units (also known as $SO_2$ scrubbers) on coal power plants.[16] In each year from 2006 to 2008, China installed around 100 GWe of scrubber capacity, more than is currently in place on the entire US coal fleet. The scrubber installation was mandated by China's 11th Five-Year Plan, which was remarkable for being the first serious effort to incorporate environmental factors into China's development planning. (Xu described how public backlash in China over the government's perceived poor handling of the SARS health crisis in 2002–2003 led the country's new leadership to conclude that non-economic factors, such as environmental degradation, could threaten the government's legitimacy just as poor economic performance could.)[17] Several factors facilitated China's push into scrubbers, including the fact that the vast majority of electric power plants in China are the property of state-owned power companies, as well as the ability of Chinese companies to manufacture scrubbers at low cost.

Mandating scrubber installation was only the first step in reducing $SO_2$ emissions, however, and not even the most difficult one. It was more challenging to make sure they were actually used properly. In 2007, China's State Environmental Protection Administration announced based on field inspections that fewer than 40% of scrubbers were "officially ready and running reliably and continuously."[18] An independent study by MIT researchers in 2007 confirmed that many power plants were still emitting high levels of $SO_2$ despite having had scrubbers installed. Since then, China's government seems to have significantly increased the rate and effectiveness of scrubber use through a combination of technology steps (installation of continuous emissions monitoring systems), incentives (a price premium for electricity generated with the scrubber operating more than 90% of the time), increased penalties for non-operation of scrubbers, and generally stepped-up inspections of power plant environmental performance.[19] These measures have helped substantially reduce $SO_2$ emissions from the power sector. The successful implementation of these various steps required sustained commitment from the government as well as learning over time by environmental regulators.

The case of China demonstrates that local pollution from large coal-fired power plants can be tamed to a significant degree where there is the political will to do so, though the process may take time. Smaller sources like industrial boilers, and much smaller sources like residential stoves, are more difficult for governments to control, which is part of why these sources are currently responsible for a disproportionate share of PM2.5 in China.

India is at an earlier stage when it comes to institutional capacity for environmental regulation. The government first imposed limits on $SO_x$, $NO_x$, and particulates from power plants in December 2015.[20] All new power plants that came online after January 1, 2017 were supposed to have required pollution control technologies in place by December 2017, but none of them actually met this deadline.[21] Prescribed environmental retrofits of older power plants had also not occurred. (The head of an electricity industry organization argued that the technology upgrades required would be expensive and that renewable energy would help India reduce emissions.)[22] The government of India seems to have conceded that installation on these plants of scrubbers and other mandated technologies is not imminent, and it has been criticized for the lack of enforcement actions to drive compliance.

India is not as far along the economic development trajectory as China, which puts it in a more difficult spot. China is fully electrified, whereas in 2014 only about 80% of India's population had access to electricity, and often not reliably.[23] The government of India is reluctant to enforce environmental rules if this means shutting down power plants. But there is also the basic problem that the environmental regulator does not yet have the power or capability to enforce its dictates in the face of competing interests. As an example, even though the Central Pollution Control Board argued for maintaining the original deadlines for pollution controls, the Central Electricity Authority supported a delay.[24]

It took China's environmental regulator some time to grow in effectiveness and political sway; the process won't happen overnight in India. That said, public pressure may start to shift the playing field in favor of environmental protection in India, just as it has in China. India's nascent air pollution regulations have already started to generate interest in pollution control and monitoring technologies inside the country, and the momentum may pick up in other respects as well.[25]

Many countries lag behind India in both grid development and establishment of a regulatory framework for air pollution. If these countries decide to opt for coal-based power, they will also need to develop the institutional capacity for air quality regulation, and that will take time.

Regulating greenhouse gases adds a whole new level of challenge. Choking smog outside the door is a more immediate call to action than the less tangible and immediate threat of climate change impacts, and air pollution control technologies are much cheaper than technologies to capture and store greenhouse gas emissions. Environmental regulations that lead to the installation of air pollution control technologies on coal-fired power plants are a major positive for health, but they don't address the climate change problem, and in some cases they might even decrease the perceived urgency around replacing coal with zero- or low-carbon energy sources.

### Environmental groups versus coal

Environmental groups have used various tactics to try to diminish the role of coal (and other fossil fuels) in the global energy system, with varying results. One of the most sophisticated efforts has been the Sierra Club's "Beyond Coal" campaign, which has organized against coal in the United States for over ten years.[26] Essentially, the Sierra Club has sought to exert pressure through every stakeholder process and leverage point that is available in a large, complex democracy. Journalist Michael Grunwald detailed how the Sierra Club challenged US coal plants, new and existing, using any vulnerability they could find.[27] In one instance, this involved leveraging endangered species protections for an endangered clover. In another, it meant arguing that required environmental upgrades for a particular coal-fired power plant would be more expensive to electricity ratepayers than switching to a non-coal alternative like natural gas. The Sierra Club sought to raise barriers along the coal supply chain that would make coal more costly, with railroads that transport coal being a particular target. For example, the organization sued to force rail operators to study measures that would reduce coal dust losses and associated water pollution from open-top rail cars.[28]

As discussed in the previous chapter, transportation can be a weak link in the coal value chain – and thus an effective link for environmentalists to attack. In the early 2010s, US coal producers set their sights on the export of Powder River Basin (PRB) coal from Wyoming (and to a lesser extent Montana) to Asia through new terminals that would be built in Washington and/or Oregon. The concern of environmentalists was that these proposed terminals could help the US fully exploit its massive PRB coal reserves and realize its potential to become the "Saudi Arabia of coal" (i.e., a giant exporter), presumably increasing total coal use worldwide. (As it turns out, the effects of an expansion in US export capacity on global coal use are surprisingly complex to model.)[29]

At the time of writing, the original six proposed port projects had all been blocked or canceled. Deteriorating project economics in the face of falling global coal prices were probably the most important culprit (though prices have recently recovered to a significant degree), but fierce and coordinated environmental opposition probably played a role as well. Environmental groups fought the proposed terminals in multiple venues on multiple grounds – including the risks of local coal dust releases, increased rail traffic, violation of Native American rights, and climate change impacts. The pattern is a common one: project economics are the first-order driver of outcomes, but environmental opposition can worsen economic prospects enough for developers to seek other options.

A core insight of the modern environmental movement is that it isn't always necessary to explicitly block a disfavored technology like coal. Simply making coal more expensive – and its regulatory environment more risky and unpredictable – in comparison to competing options can influence how much coal is mined, transported, and used. Environmentalists have sought to do this by confronting coal at every step of the value chain: by challenging environmental and safety issues associated with mining, by making rail transport of coal more difficult and expensive, by trying to block construction of coal ports, and by trying to block new coal power plants and shut down existing ones. Often these groups engage with policy goals and forums that are not explicitly environmental in nature, as when the Sierra Club argued against coal-fired power plant retrofits on the grounds that they would be more expensive for ratepayers than new gas-fired plants.

Not all countries are tolerant of legal action and advocacy by non-governmental organizations (NGOs). In such cases, NGOs may seek to effect change in a less confrontational way through information provision. The information NGOs provide – for example in the form of studies of the health risks of air pollution – can help build public support for emissions controls or a reduction in the role of coal. Sometimes central governments struggle to achieve their own environmental priorities because of resistance by interests opposed to tighter environmental rules. In such cases, governments may view environmental NGOs as provisional allies. At the same time, it can be a delicate balance for NGOs. India received attention in 2015 for trying to curtail the activities of NGOs in a variety of areas, including Greenpeace India, which advocated strongly against coal.[30]

The case of China illustrates some of the tensions around provision of environmental data. China's government long chafed at the US Embassy's dissemination of independent air quality data, and in 2014 it ordered mobile apps to stop using this data.[31] At the same time, improvement in air quality was a genuine government priority, and regulators wanted to avoid the perception that they were covering up inconvenient data. China's government has become progressively more open in sharing air quality information. The efforts of China-based branches of international environmental groups to provide information on coal and pollution seem to be cautiously welcomed by the central government, as long as they stay within certain boundaries.

Information provision could boost public support for cleaning the air – and help the central government build pressure on provincial and local governments to reduce emissions.

At an international level, environmental groups have tried to raise consciousness about the large and continuing role of coal in the world energy supply. The Natural Resources Defense Council (NRDC) and World Wildlife Fund (WWF) have collected information on the financing sources for coal plants. Greenpeace has supported and published studies on the air pollution impacts of coal in countries around the world. Coalswarm, Greenpeace, and the Sierra Club have helped support an online tracker of all significant coal power plants that are proposed or under construction around the world.[32] The idea is that shining a light on the pipeline of new coal power plants being developed worldwide will call attention to the environmental risks posed by coal far into the future and help mobilize efforts against specific projects.

At the opposite end of the tactical spectrum from provision of objective information are efforts by environmental groups to frame the fight against coal as a moral crusade. One of the leading organizations taking this approach has been 350.org, so named for the goal of reducing $CO_2$ concentrations in the atmosphere below 350ppm in order to mitigate the worst climate change risks. 350.org and other environmental groups with a similar mindset take the position that most of the world's fossil fuel reserves – and especially its coal – are "unburnable carbon," meaning they cannot ever be used lest we expose the Earth and all its inhabitants to catastrophic climate change. Making any further investments in fossil fuel extraction and use is therefore seen as both morally untenable and financially unwise, as the performance of companies involved in fossil fuel activities will presumably suffer when the world finally realizes these fossil fuels cannot be used. (In a 2015 paper in *Nature*, McGlade and Ekins modeled how the assumption of a strict 2°C limit on global temperature rise would affect which fossil fuel reserves could actually be extracted and burned.)[33]

The fossil fuel divestment movement has been one of the most visible instruments of 350.org and allied organizations. The idea is to pressure university endowments and pension funds to sell off any holdings in companies that are in the business of producing fossil fuels. Concern among students about the Earth's climate future has given this movement particular energy on university campuses, with students pushing administrators at colleges across the United States to divest. The movement has touted some apparent successes. In 2014, Stanford University President John Hennessy announced that the university would shed all direct holdings in companies whose primary business was coal extraction. "The university's review has concluded that coal is one of the most carbon-intensive methods of energy generation and that other sources can be readily substituted for it," Hennessy said.[34] Ultimately, though, Stanford's move was more symbolic than substantive. The university's "direct" holdings in coal were negligible, and it did not make any pledge to restrict the holdings of the many diversified funds in which the endowment was invested. In 2016, the Stanford Board of Trustees explicitly rejected a call for the university to divest from fossil fuels more broadly, stating that "oil and gas remain integral components of the global economy, essential to the daily lives of billions of people in both developed and emerging economies."[35]

California passed a law in 2015 that required two major state pension funds, the California Public Employees'

Retirement System (CalPERS) and the California State Teachers' Retirement System (CalSTRS), to divest from coal.[36] When the law was passed, the stocks of US coal companies were trading at very low levels, so the pension funds perhaps appeared to be sacrificing little. Many share prices later rebounded, most notably that of Peabody Energy, which declared bankruptcy in 2016 and then re-emerged from it. This, of course, is the concern fund managers have – that socially based restrictions like a prohibition on coal investment will ultimately harm returns, with a negative effect on the health of the state retirement system.

Arguably the most significant divestment thus far has been that of Norway's Government Pension Fund Global, which invests the country's oil and gas revenues to benefit future generations of Norwegians. In 2015, Norway's parliament directed the fund, which is currently worth around $1 trillion, to divest from enterprises with more than 30% of their business in coal. Norway's finance ministry calculated at the time that this could affect $9–10 billion of the fund's investments.[37] Still, Norway has thus far resisted pressure to divest from oil and gas.[38]

These examples illustrate two phenomena observed thus far when it comes to fossil fuel divestment. First, coal appears to be "low-hanging fruit," in that divestment from coal is far easier than divestment from oil and gas. For this reason, coal may continue to attract more divestment moves. Whether these end up having a material financial effect on the global coal industry remains to be seen. Second, even the coal divestments have not been absolute. For example, both Stanford and Norway effectively limited their divestments to enterprises whose primary business was coal-related. As *Agence France-Presse* pointed out, the world's three largest coal producers – Anglo American, BHP Billiton, and Glencore – were not affected by Norway's divestment because they are massive mining conglomerates for which coal represents less than 30% of overall revenue.[39]

An even more direct way to communicate the idea that coal shouldn't be used is to engage in confrontational protests that try to shut down coal-fired power plants. This is a tactic long used to protest nuclear power, but it's relatively new for coal. In fact, Germany's anti-coal protests, in which thousands of protesters have tried to interrupt coal operations, trace their heritage directly to the anti-nuclear movement that has been so successful in that country.[40] A variety of other environmental groups have staged attention-grabbing anti-coal protests around the world. Greenpeace was behind several visible incidents, including one in 2008 in which protesters painted "Go Solar" in giant letters down a smokestack at the Swanbank coal power station in Queensland, Australia. Greenpeace, 350.org, and other organizations coordinated "Break Free from Fossil Fuels" demonstrations around the world in May 2016.

A significant limitation of these tactics is their limited applicability in countries whose governments are intolerant of unapproved NGO activity and public demonstrations. Despite their central importance where coal is concerned, China and India were noticeably absent from the list of countries where "Break Free" protests took place.

### International finance and international climate politics

In recent years, environmental organizations have tried to discourage public financing of coal-fired power plants, which are typically multi-billion-dollar projects. Financial institutions, including international ones, play a key role in developing power projects. Important actors include

venerable multilateral development banks like the World
Bank, newer lending institutions like the China-led Asian
Infrastructure Investment Bank (AIIB), export credit agencies like the Japan Bank for International Cooperation
(JBIC) and Export-Import Bank of China, and a variety
of other public and private financial entities including
domestic banks. Under the Obama administration, the
government of the United States, in conjunction with a
number of European countries, pushed for an agreement
among OECD nations to end public financing for coal-
fired generators. This was initially resisted by Japan, South
Korea, and Australia. Japan and South Korea are major
importers of coal and exporters of coal power plant technology, and Australia is a major exporter of coal. However,
these countries eventually supported a joint statement in
2015, effective January 1, 2017, to restrict OECD public
financing to ultra-supercritical coal plants (such as those
built by Japanese and Korean companies), except in the
case of "poorer, developing countries."[41] The World Bank
had already agreed in 2013 to restrict financing for new
coal-fired projects to countries with "no feasible alternatives" to coal.[42]

In 2017, the Trump administration reversed the US
government's position on public financing for coal,
instructing US representatives to the World Bank and
other multilateral financial institutions to undo the Obama
administration's stance and support public financing of
overseas coal plants.[43] However, this move seems unlikely
to have any effect on the position of the World Bank, which
if anything has strengthened its opposition to coal (and,
increasingly, other fossil fuels).[44]

It is not yet clear how much impact these moves by multilateral financial institutions will have. Ultra-supercritical
plants are probably one of the more competitive niches for

Japanese and Korean (and Chinese) companies anyway, and the definition of "poorer, developing countries" could be interpreted broadly enough to encompass most prospective markets for new coal power stations. A study of 22 coal-fired power deals in Indonesia that closed between January 2010 and March 2017 showed that export credit agencies played a role in 64% of them, with JBIC involved in five deals and the Export-Import Bank of China involved in seven deals.[45] More broadly, China, Japan, South Korea, and Germany have been major lenders to coal projects, with China increasingly playing the leading role in supporting coal around the world.[46] Even if OECD lenders curtail their involvement in financing coal power, Chinese and other non-OECD institutions would not be so bound – nor would non-OECD-led multilateral development banks.

There are plenty of providers of coal technology too. Japan has been a leader in supplying advanced, efficient coal technology to growing markets like Southeast Asia,[47] but it appears China has surpassed it. According to data from the Global Coal Plant Tracker put together by various environmental organizations, Chinese companies will build almost half of the coal plants installed over the next decade, with a large share of these being outside China.[48] If anything, China's efforts to contain its own domestic coal use will create even more impetus for these companies to seek business abroad. The strong business incentives of Chinese and non-Chinese purveyors of coal plant technology are an obstacle to environmentalists' effort to stem the expansion of coal-fired power around the world.

Debates around international coal power financing contain in microcosm the basic energy security versus environmental quality dilemma around coal. Back in 2010, the World Bank had to decide whether to loan over $3 billion to South Africa's state power company Eskom to help it build a massive coal-fired power plant known as Medupi. The need appeared dire, in particular because other financing options had dried up in the wake of the 2008 global financial crisis. South Africa had been experiencing serious electricity shortages for the previous several years, the result of longtime underinvestment in new generation capacity, unstable government policy for the electricity sector, and management deficiencies in Eskom, including in the area of coal procurement.[49] The worst blackouts, in 2008, left homes without power for many hours a day and disrupted commercial and industrial enterprises across the country. Even South Africa's economically crucial mining industry (of which coal mining is a key component) was forced to curtail its electricity use.

The South African government portrayed the roughly 4,800 MW of power that Medupi would provide (along with another 4,800 MW that would come from Medupi's partner plant, Kusile) as absolutely essential. Discussing the importance of the World Bank loan, South Africa's Public Enterprises Minister Barbara Hogan said, "If we do not have that power in our system, then we can say goodbye to our economy and to our country."[50] Hogan further stressed that it was not only South Africa's future at risk: "South Africa generates more than 60% of all electricity produced in Sub-Saharan Africa. Electricity shortfalls in South Africa would hinder the economic development of the region. Botswana, Lesotho, Namibia, Swaziland, and Zimbabwe rely on Eskom for their electricity."[51]

Environmental groups concerned about climate change were just as insistent that the loan for Medupi should not be granted. As discussed previously, burning coal produces significant quantities of carbon dioxide, a potent and long-lived greenhouse gas, and coal combustion is the largest contributor to $CO_2$ emissions from the energy sector. The

Medupi plant was projected to emit roughly 25 million tonnes of $CO_2$ every year when fully operational.[52] Bobby Peek, director of South African nonprofit groundWork, framed the prospective loan in the following terms: "This investment into coal in South Africa is a clear indication that the World Bank is not truthful in its commitments to climate change."[53] The Environmental Defense Fund, the Sierra Club, and Friends of the Earth lined up with South African civic groups against the loan.[54]

Some nods were made to environmental concerns in the project design for Medupi. Of the $3.75 billion loan package, $260 million was designated for renewable energy.[55] The coal-fired power plant was designed with "supercritical" technology, which results in higher efficiency (and thus lower emissions) than the "subcritical" design typical of existing coal plants. South Africa also committed to retiring old coal plants more quickly and to advancing technology for carbon capture and storage (CCS) that could capture the $CO_2$ from future power plants and dispose of it underground.[56]

In the end, the South African government's argument about the need for energy won out over the anti-coal environmental arguments, and the loan was approved. The United States government under Obama abstained from the vote, as did the governments of the Netherlands, the United Kingdom, and Italy.

The international politics of coal often devolve into this kind of argument about whether climate goals or development goals should have top priority. Developing country governments insist, quite reasonably, that they have a right to develop just like rich countries did, even if this means burning coal. They point out that their per capita energy consumption and greenhouse gas emissions are far below those of rich countries. Those on the other side of the debate argue that most of the increase in global greenhouse gas emissions going forward will come from developing countries. This is also true.

Environmental advocates sometimes finesse away the climate–development tension by arguing that intermittent renewable energy is already, or soon will be, economically competitive with coal, even without stronger environmental policy. According to this argument, developing countries will be better off economically if they forgo new coal plant construction in favor of wind and solar. This means that developing countries are being irrational by continuing to build coal rather than wind or solar, perhaps because governments and regulators have been captured by coal interests. The argument that wind and/or solar are already more economic than coal for delivering electricity at scale, even without accounting for the full social costs of coal, is questionable, as I discuss in Chapter 5.

The fact that coal is such a *bête noire* in international climate discussions can give rise to a disconnect whereby countries highlight their actions on renewable energy and downplay their planned increases in coal production and use. In the run-up to the Paris Climate Conference in 2015, India was attracting unfavorable attention for its planned growth in domestic coal production. As soon as it released ambitious plans for expanding renewable capacity, including a planned 100 GW of new solar slated to come online by 2022, the political pressure it faced in the climate arena decreased markedly. In another example, Germany was hailed as an environmental leader for its substantial increases in renewable energy even as it expanded coal supply and missed greenhouse gas emissions targets. The "German model" of significant generation from both coal and renewable energy, which India seems to be following as well, is counterproductive if the goal is least-cost emissions reduction. At the same time, it has a certain political logic. Adding renewable energy is the best way to get credit for being green, and maintaining or adding coal generation is a cheap way to make sure the lights stay on.

## The impact of environmental advocacy

The anti-coal environmental movement has been most successful where alternatives to coal are least expensive and most readily available. The best example has been the Sierra Club's effort to target the coal value chain in the United States. The availability of cheap and plentiful natural gas delivered via a well-developed pipeline network has been the primary factor in the reduction in coal use in the US, but focused anti-coal efforts by the Sierra Club and other environmental groups to fight coal in every possible venue have also played a role at the margin. Environmental campaigns increase cost and uncertainty around coal, so they can be effective if the economic gap between coal and the next cheapest alternative is not huge. (To the extent that anti-fracking or other anti-gas campaigns raise the price of gas, they may end up working at cross-purposes to environmentalists' anti-coal efforts.)

While it is difficult to quantify the effect of information provision, it seems likely it has had some impact. As detailed earlier in this chapter, significant majorities of people around the world are now sensitized to the risks of climate change, even if this hasn't for the most part translated into stringent carbon pricing or other climate policy. More coal-specific analysis and policy outreach, including on the global coal fleet, its growth, and the pollution implications, have drawn attention to the environmental implications of relying on coal-fired power.

More confrontational environmental advocacy strategies – and especially the fossil fuel divestment movement – have garnered significant media attention, although the concrete impact on policy and investment is not easy to assess at this point. It is also difficult to quantify the impact of international efforts to squeeze off coal financing. Even as the World Bank and the Asian Development Bank have mostly eschewed support for new coal-fired power plant developments, other money and expertise is stepping into the void. Chinese banks and engineering firms appear to be displacing Japanese ones as the leading developers of overseas coal plants even as China tries to contain coal use at home. China may be starting to plateau in coal use, but Southeast Asia and other regions are just getting started, and Chinese firms are certainly helping coal along.

## Conclusion

Policies that more completely incorporate into energy prices the environmental externalities of energy production and use (the negative environmental impacts of energy that no one fully pays for at present) would make coal less attractive relative to alternatives. Historically, governments have focused more on environmental regulation after most citizens' basic needs for income and employment are met, and the demand for cleaner, healthier air and water increases. China, for example, has started to tackle air pollution concerns more aggressively, with rules that limit sulfur dioxide emissions from power plants and even direct restrictions on coal burning in and around Beijing and other major cities. India may be following in China's footsteps, but it is at an earlier stage in the process of developing the political will and regulatory capability to act effectively. In both developing and developed countries, political support is higher for tackling the immediately visible problem of air pollution, as compared with the less visible, longer-term issue of climate change. Still, majorities of survey respondents in virtually all countries viewed climate change as a serious issue, and it seems likely that climate policies will tighten over time.

Environmental groups have opposed coal using various tactics. The Sierra Club's "Beyond Coal" campaign was one notable, and fairly effective, campaign that fought coal in the United States for over a decade by taking advantage of all available stakeholder processes. Environmental groups have to tread more carefully in countries with less democratic systems, but some have managed to play a role in such countries by disseminating information about air quality and health impacts of burning coal. One of the more aggressive anti-coal movements aims to get large pension funds and university endowments to divest from coal (and fossil fuels more generally). There have been some prominent announcements of funds divesting from coal – and coal is probably the "low-hanging fruit" among fossil fuels in that it has a higher carbon footprint *and* is easier to divest from than oil and gas – but it is difficult to tell if these efforts have had a significant financial effect on coal companies thus far.

With the support of their funding countries, prominent multilateral development banks, most notably the World Bank, have moved away from financing coal projects on environmental grounds. Still, it seems unlikely that this will choke off all capital to coal power projects around the world, especially as the locus of coal financing and project development shifts from Japan to China.

Environmental activism has probably had some effect on coal at the margins, especially where economically competitive alternatives to coal are available, as in North America.

It is also possible that anti-coal campaigns will start to have a cumulative effect in diminishing the public acceptance of coal use around the world. Still, it is likely that alternatives to coal will have to become significantly cheaper as well, in order for coal to lose its dominant position in global electricity generation. The next chapter considers the advantages and disadvantages of these alternatives, and what would have to occur for them to outcompete coal in the marketplace.

CHAPTER FIVE

# Alternatives to Coal

Where alternatives exist that are already broadly cheaper than coal and functionally equivalent – for example, in North America, where cheap natural gas means gas-fired power is less expensive than coal-fired power – market forces alone will lead to the replacement of coal with other energy sources. This is the phenomenon of "BTU arbitrage" discussed in Chapter 1: all else equal, and not considering environmental or other social concerns, markets will supply the cheapest available source of energy. Of course, if the policy framework under which energy markets operate *does* factor environmental or other social concerns into the energy price, markets will take these factors into account as well, as occurs for example when there is a carbon price.

Power plants have fixed costs, which are incurred regardless of whether the plant operates, and variable costs, which are incurred only when the plant runs and generates energy. The characteristic balance between fixed costs and variable costs differs across energy options. The most significant fixed cost for a power plant is usually the capital cost of building the plant itself, which is amortized over time as the plant pays back the loans that financed its construction. The most significant variable cost for most non-renewable power plants is the cost of fuel: for example, coal or natural gas. For a renewable generator like a wind or solar facility, variable costs are close to zero because no fuel is needed; almost all of the cost is the fixed cost of building the facility. Nuclear power plants have some variable cost from the uranium fuel used to power them, but the significant majority of the total cost is still the very high fixed cost of construction. Coal power plants are next along the continuum, with relatively high fixed costs of construction (but not as high as for nuclear) and relatively cheap fuel (but not as cheap as for nuclear). Finally, natural-gas-fired power plants are at the other extreme: fairly cheap to build but with relatively high variable costs because natural gas is expensive in most regions.

In a world of tightening environmental standards, which energy alternatives are best positioned to replace coal on cost and other dimensions? The answer seems to depend on whom you ask. "Wind and solar," say those for whom green is synonymous with renewable. "Nuclear," say people who think intermittency (the fact that wind and solar are not available on demand) will prove too tough a nut to crack if wind and solar come to represent a large share of generation. "Natural gas," say pragmatists who think coal's most direct competitor in power generation has the best chance of eating into coal's dominant position, even if gas only reduces carbon emissions by a factor of two relative to coal. "Clean coal," says the coal industry, where "clean coal" could mean coal-fired power plants with control technologies to remove local pollutants, or plants with carbon capture and storage (CCS), or both. "All of the above," say those who argue that a balanced portfolio is least costly.

Relative costs of these various technologies can shift quickly. Natural gas prices in North America dropped sharply with the advent of new techniques for shale gas extraction. Solar costs have fallen steadily over the last decade. Also, each energy supply alternative has advantages and disadvantages beyond cost alone.

This chapter considers how coal stacks up against several important alternatives, and what it would take for each alternative to start displacing new coal power projects in a significant way. The chapter also discusses how different kinds of energy and environmental policies would differentially affect coal versus various coal alternatives.

Several alternatives to coal are not discussed here. Hydro and geothermal are both valuable renewable resources, with the important advantage that their energy is not intermittent like wind or solar (assuming, in the case of hydro, that there is plenty of water behind the dam). However, good hydro and geothermal resources are only available in certain locations around the world, and many of the most promising sites have already been developed. Geothermal can also be a relatively expensive resource to develop, which helps explain, for example, why Indonesia, with plentiful cheap coal, has not tapped even more of its significant geothermal resource than it has.

I also don't devote a special section to biomass energy, in large part because of the complexities around its environmental impact. Energy from biomass can certainly be renewable – and low-carbon – in theory. In the European Union, biomass met an estimated 10% of total primary energy demand in 2016.[1] The challenge is that one has to be extremely careful about how the biomass is sourced, or else biomass energy can become a serious environmental negative. If agricultural waste is used, or if fuel crops are replanted after they are burned for energy, energy from biomass can be carbon-neutral (or even carbon-negative if more carbon is sequestered in the cycle than is released). However, there is a crucial caveat when plants are grown for fuel, which is that existing forests were not cleared in order to make way for the fuel crop. If the carbon locked in pre-existing forests is released to the atmosphere prior to the cultivation of fuel crops, it can create a "carbon debt" for which even many years of carbon-neutral biomass use are insufficient to compensate. Even when consumers of biomass energy strive to avoid this problem, there is a risk that their demand for biomass fuel can create incentives for deforestation around the world.

I do not explicitly consider energy efficiency and conservation here. While extremely important, energy efficiency and conservation are not energy supply alternatives to coal. Rather, they are ways to limit the need for expanding the energy supply in the first place, and as such they should be pursued to the greatest extent possible. Energy that is not generated cannot cause pollution or climate change or any other social problem. Improving energy efficiency – of vehicles, household appliances, industrial processes, commercial operations, and all other energy uses – can help reduce energy demand growth in developing countries and overall energy demand in developed ones. It can even help make high-quality energy services accessible where they weren't before. For example, advances in low-power LED lighting technology have led to the spread of solar and battery-powered lights in off-grid areas.

Demand-side market incentives can play an important role in limiting the need for new energy supply. In electricity grids, sufficient generation capacity needs to be available to meet peak demand, but peak demand can be reduced substantially if consumers are given dynamic price signals that encourage them to consume less at peak times. As the supply mix comes to incorporate more and more intermittent renewables like wind and solar, dynamic pricing can encourage consumers to use less electricity when the wind isn't blowing and the sun isn't shining, which ultimately means less need for new power plants.

The comparisons of energy sources below are mostly

focused on electricity generation, but there is some discussion of industrial uses as well. Later in this chapter, we focus specifically on the special role of coking coal in steelmaking, and why it is not so easily or cheaply eliminated.

## Coal vs. nuclear

Coal and nuclear power plants have a lot in common. They are both built large to rely on economies of scale. They both have high fixed costs to build (though those of nuclear are substantially higher) and relatively low fuel costs. They are both highly unpopular. They both operate most efficiently when allowed to run continuously in "baseload" mode, because they both have substantial costs associated with starting and stopping.

A major difference between coal and nuclear is that nuclear doesn't emit local pollutants or greenhouse gases. In addition, nuclear has a much better track record than coal when it comes to safety and accidents (though concern about the potential magnitude of an individual nuclear accident is understandable). Historical fatality rates from nuclear power accidents have been several orders of magnitude lower than those from coal mining, and the disparity grows substantially larger if mortality from air pollution is taken into account.[2]

The public acceptance problem for nuclear is a major obstacle to its expansion around the world. Distaste for nuclear is not uniform among countries. A cross-country survey by WorldPublicOpinion.org in 2008 suggested that nuclear was relatively more accepted in China, India, South Korea, and Poland than in Germany, Indonesia, Russia, Thailand, and the United States.[3] It is perhaps unsurprising, then, that China, India, and South Korea are among the few countries that have been focused on expanding nuclear power. China is adding more nuclear capacity than any other country. However, anti-nuclear sentiment in China has grown stronger since the 2011 Fukushima Daiichi accident in Japan, despite the tight lid the government keeps on dissent.[4] Public opinion on nuclear in South Korea has also grown more mixed in the wake of both Fukushima and a domestic scandal involving falsification of safety documents for nuclear power plant components.[5]

Nuclear is especially unpopular in Germany. A 2017 survey commissioned by Danish renewable energy company Ørsted corroborated the results of the 2008 survey by WorldPublicOpinion.org, showing that even more German respondents wanted their country to use less nuclear than to use less coal (69% vs. 67%).[6] It makes sense, therefore, that politicians in Germany have prioritized the phase-out of nuclear power. However, this has negated much of the greenhouse gas emissions benefit that would otherwise have come from Germany's aggressive additions of renewable energy capacity. As nuclear has left the generation mix in Germany, coal-fired capacity has picked up the slack.

There are certainly unique and legitimate concerns about nuclear energy. It produces radioactive waste that needs to be safely stored for hundreds or thousands of years. There is a risk that fuel could be diverted to manufacture nuclear weapons. Accidents or deliberate sabotage could expose populations to deadly levels of radioactivity. Even the best technological safeguards don't entirely eliminate the risk of accidents. Regulator and operator complacency and error remain a possibility for any industrial process. In the United States, the Institute of Nuclear Power Operations, or INPO, was formed in the wake of the 1979 Three Mile Island accident to drive continuous improvement in operational and safety performance, and it has had a significant positive impact in these areas.[7]

For all these very real concerns, nuclear often seems to be held to a loftier standard than coal, at least when it comes to historical health and safety statistics. And it is not just public concern per se that makes nuclear unpromising as a greener substitute for coal. It is also the fact that public acceptance problems frequently translate into regulatory uncertainty and delays, and in turn, greatly increased costs. For a facility as complex and capital-intensive as a nuclear power plant, delays are absolutely deadly to project finances. The classic example of this occurred in the US nuclear power industry. After Three Mile Island, "safety became an obsession," as James Cook put it in a comprehensive and nuanced 1985 article in *Forbes*. "The NRC [Nuclear Regulatory Commission] promulgated hundreds of new safety regulations between 1978 and 1983 to cope with contingencies ranging from earthquakes to missile strikes."[8] Some of these new regulations were justified, and others were probably not, but in any event the delays that resulted from these regulatory add-ons were financially devastating to the industry and marked the beginning of the end of the golden age of nuclear capacity additions in the United States. (Utility mismanagement, including overestimation of new capacity needs and underestimation of costs, played a major role in the debacle too.)

Over thirty years later, the landscape for nuclear power looks not much improved. Delays and cost overruns are endemic, and financial perils abound for the companies involved. Construction was stopped on two reactors in South Carolina, and costs ballooned for the last two reactors still being built in the US, in Georgia.[9] The experience in Georgia and elsewhere helped push Toshiba's nuclear subsidiary Westinghouse into bankruptcy. Olkiluoto Unit 3 in Finland, built by France's Areva, has been a decade late and a factor of three over budget, which helped spur the French government to bail out Areva and force it to merge into state-owned French power company EDF.[10] Earlier-stage projects by Areva in France and the UK also faced delays, financial difficulties, and additional regulatory scrutiny.[11] (Areva's experiences in China were somewhat more favorable.)[12] Both Westinghouse's and Areva's reactors were new designs intended to have significantly better safety characteristics, and these safety-related enhancements proved more expensive than anticipated.

Nuclear has simply become too big a financial gamble for private companies to take, and the challenge is worse where there are competitive electricity markets. The economic case for nuclear is even shakier in the absence of a significant carbon price or other strong policy valuing the environmental benefits of nuclear relative to coal. It's no surprise that the most successful historical build-out of nuclear power, in France, was the result of a concerted government push rather than pure market forces. China's government-led approach explains why it is able to move fastest on nuclear today.

For the above reasons, it seems unlikely that nuclear will be a formidable competitor to coal any time soon, except in special cases like China. Even in China it is difficult to envision nuclear growing large enough to displace major shares of coal.

One wildcard that could conceivably change this picture in the longer term would be breakthroughs in advanced reactor technologies and small nuclear reactors. A number of nuclear energy startup companies, universities, and national laboratories in North America are exploring advanced reactor technologies that could in theory be safer, smaller, cheaper, and more efficient. The think tank Third Way surveyed the advanced nuclear landscape in North America in 2016 and found 60 advanced nuclear development projects.[13] Small modular reactors (SMRs) might in theory offer some advantages relative to current reactor designs. Cost reductions might be possible from building reactors in a manufacturing line rather than as huge, expensive, site-specific one-offs. Reactors that are amenable to factory fabrication might avoid the problem of construction delays, which have been nuclear's fatal flaw from a financial perspective. SMRs, with standardized safety and waste handling, could finally give the public a level of comfort with nuclear power that it does not have at present. The smaller sizes of SMRs could conceivably make them viable for industrial heating and power applications as well as the central power stations in which nuclear is packaged today.

For all the theoretical potential of advanced reactor types and SMRs, the fact is that these concepts are not new. If it were easy to develop them into cost-effective energy solutions, it would have been done already. The jury is still out on whether they will end up playing an important role in the energy mix of the future. At the very least, significant deployment is probably a decade or more away.[14]

## Coal vs. natural gas

Natural gas is coal's most direct competitor today. Combined cycle gas turbine (CCGT) power plants are cheap to build and efficient to operate. They emit minimal $SO_x$ and particulates and only about half the $CO_2$ of coal plants. Natural gas is a cleaner fuel for heat and power in industrial applications. (Natural gas *cannot* easily substitute for coking coal in producing the pig iron needed to make steel.)

The traditional disadvantage of gas relative to coal is that gas is a more expensive, less readily available fuel. Part of this is the cost of extracting gas from the ground, but another big contribution is the cost of building specialized transportation infrastructure. Whereas coal can be shipped fairly cheaply on rail cars or bulk carrier ships, natural gas needs expensive pipelines or liquefied natural gas (LNG) infrastructure. Long-distance transport projects are multi-billion-dollar propositions. Pipelines for gas need compressors all along their routes. LNG shipment requires a liquefaction plant, LNG tankers to transport the liquefied gas at very low temperature, and a regasification plant at the destination. Altogether, this could add \$4–6/MMBtu for shipment of gas from North America to Asia, potentially increasing the final price by a factor of two or more.

The proliferation of LNG facilities does mean that natural gas is now available in any country with a regasification terminal on its coast. Close to 20 countries export LNG; the market is wide and deep and growing. In 2016, even price wasn't much of a problem, as excess global supply pushed the average delivered price to Northeast Asia down to \$5.52/MMBtu in 2016, far lower than in years past.[15] Low delivered gas prices led to higher utilization of gas in existing power plants in Asia. India's government, for example, pushed to restart gas-fired power plants that had been idled. If Asian buyers trusted that average gas prices would stay that low forever, there would have been significant coal-to-gas switching and gas plant construction in Asia. The trouble is, they didn't trust these low prices, and with some justification. Asian gas prices have traditionally been linked to oil, and they shot up in the 2000s alongside oil prices. The price of gas delivered to Japan has topped \$15/MMBtu for significant periods. At that gas price, it would take an extremely high carbon price for a gas-fired power plant to beat coal on cost.

The dynamics of natural gas markets have changed significantly since the late 2000s, though. The US and

Australia have brought major new supplies of natural gas online. It looks like the "shale gas revolution" in North America will persist for some time, and eventually other countries may start to develop their shale resources too. Oil prices dropped steeply starting in 2014, so oil-inked gas prices went lower too. Pricing formulas became less rigid, with at least some movement away from oil linkage. All these factors might seem to provide some comfort in theory that natural gas could be a relatively affordable fuel over the long term.

There are other concerns beside price and availability that drive the perception on the part of planners and investors that gas is less energy secure. Major emerging markets like China and India have significantly more domestic coal than domestic gas, and part of the resistance to gas may be an inherent feeling that foreign imports are less trustworthy. As discussed in Chapter 2, the assumption that domestic resources are energy secure is highly questionable. In practice, major energy disruptions have arisen most commonly due to the combination of severe weather or natural disasters, infrastructure vulnerabilities, and institutional failures, rather than actions by a foreign supplier.

One energy security argument sometimes made in favor of coal is that it is easier to store than natural gas. This argument is often overstated. It is true that gas requires specialized storage. The most cost-effective way to store large quantities of gas is underground, in geological formations with special properties that ensure the gas will not leak out, such as depleted oil and gas fields, aquifers, and salt caverns.[16] Coal, by contrast, can be stockpiled in open fields next to power plants. The Trump administration has argued that coal (and nuclear) power plants in the US should be subsidized precisely for the energy security benefit that supposedly follows from their ability to stockpile significant quantities of fuel on site.[17] The reality is more complicated. When exposed to the elements, coal tends to oxidize over time and gain moisture, reducing its energy content. Coal stacks release fine particles, causing pollution and further loss of energy content. In addition, there is a risk of self-heating and spontaneous combustion. Covered storage that could help minimize these problems is relatively expensive. For all of these reasons – and in order to be more economically competitive – coal plant operators generally try to minimize the size of their stockpiles to the extent possible.

Gas markets and pricing are dysfunctional in many countries, which has been another factor limiting the role of natural gas.[18] As discussed above, many locations still price gas based on the oil price, which has often resulted in prices so high they discourage gas use. (Natural gas expert Peter Hughes has argued persuasively that oil indexation cost gas a major niche in the power generation sector in Europe.)[19] One important reason the shale gas revolution happened in the United States is that gas in the US market is priced based on supply and demand for gas. Rising gas prices in the 2000s sent a clear signal that technological innovation in gas production would be rewarded.

Countries with domestic gas resources often price domestic gas so low – for example at the cost of extraction and transport plus some modest premium[20] – that it discourages companies from developing gas fields and making the major investments required for gas transportation, while also encouraging over-consumption of gas. There usually isn't enough of this cheap gas to go around, and favored consumers get the first crack at it. In India, this has meant politically connected fertilizer and power producers get preferential access to cheap gas while other users turn to internationally priced LNG.[21] Despite the greenhouse gas emissions advantages of gas relative to coal, India pointedly did not include natural gas in its Intended Nationally Determined Contribution (INDC) to climate change action as part of the Paris Climate Conference. This may have reflected the perception that gas is less energy-secure than coal, but it could also have represented a recognition that gas for power in India is held back by problems in the domestic gas market.

North America is one place where "the Golden Age of Gas" has definitively arrived, and where gas is now the "default fuel" instead of coal. This is thanks to the mature gas grid, gas prices that are set based on supply and demand, and, crucially, the way the shale gas revolution unlocked large supplies and lowered prices (see Box 5.1). The shale gas revolution in the United States was enabled by mature gas infrastructure and market-determined prices as well as other factors including well-understood and favorable geology, a vibrant oilfield services industry enabling rapid experimentation, and a mineral rights regime that gave property owners subsurface rights and thus the potential to benefit if hydrocarbons were found on their land.

---

**Box 5.1** The shale gas revolution

Oil and natural gas formed when organic material fell to the bottom of prehistoric seas and was heated and compressed over millions of years. "Conventional" reservoirs were created when these hydrocarbons migrated away from the source rock where they formed and into porous and permeable reservoir rock, where they were kept in place by a cap rock or other impermeable geological formation above. Large quantities of oil and gas are trapped in such reservoirs at high pressure. Once you sink a well into the reservoir, oil and/or gas will flow easily for many years.

"Unconventional gas" is natural gas that never left its source rock because the source rock permeability was too low – in other words, fluid couldn't flow easily through it. Geologists have long known there were huge quantities of gas trapped in thin shale layers in North America (and elsewhere), but until the mid- to late-2000s, it wasn't widely believed this gas could ever be extracted at a cost that would be competitive in the marketplace.

A combination of three existing technologies turned shale gas extraction into the energy game changer it has become. Advanced seismic imaging gave oil and gas operators a far more precise idea of where these thin, hydrocarbon-rich shale layers were lying. Horizontal drilling allowed operators to accurately bend their well bores sideways into these layers to extract far more gas from a single well. Hydraulic fracturing ("fracking") forced liquid into these shales at high pressure to break open paths for the gas to flow into the well.

The end result has been a vast expansion of natural gas reserves and production in North America, with a corresponding decrease in price. Shale gas reserves are sizeable in other parts of the world too, but significant production has not yet taken place. Still, the increase in North American supplies has had effects on gas price in other markets. By displacing significant quantities of LNG that would otherwise have flowed into North America, the shale gas revolution helped lower delivered LNG prices elsewhere around the world, and this effect will be accentuated as the United States becomes an important LNG exporter itself.

Unconventional gas extraction has acquired a bad reputation on the environmental front, with "fracking" attracting particular ire. There is little evidence that environmental problems in early US shale gas developments were the result of fracking per se; more likely causes were poor practices by early shale gas operators, such as a failure to properly cement the casings of wells, which could let gas migrate into aquifers or drinking water wells.

Other countries possess shale gas resources too. According to a geological assessment published in 2013 by the US Energy Information Administration, the United States ranks behind China, Argentina, and Algeria in the size of its technically recoverable shale gas resources, and just ahead of Canada and Mexico.[22] While it is not guaranteed that technically recoverable resources can be extracted economically, these estimates at least suggest that significant shale gas production may be possible outside the US. Efforts to extract shale gas elsewhere are under way, with China and Argentina being particular focal points. Large-scale success in China could have major implications for Asian energy markets, possibly sparking a more significant shift toward gas in China and reducing gas prices elsewhere in the region. However, progress on shale gas in China has been slow so far. Obstacles include difficult geology, high population density, water issues, less mature gas infrastructure and markets, and a more closed and less competitive hydrocarbons sector. China's dominant, large-scale, state-owned oil companies have less incentive to move quickly than nimble small- to medium-sized private companies did in the United States.[23]

In much of the world, there is fierce environmental opposition to the hydraulic fracturing ("fracking") technology used to make gas flow in impermeable rock (see Box 5.1). There appear to have been cases where poor construction of shale gas wells (though not fracking itself) led to contamination of drinking water wells.[24] At the same time, it's not clear unconventional gas extraction is uniquely damaging in comparison with other fossil fuel activities. Coal mining, with its acid rock drainage and other issues, probably poses more severe water risks than unconventional gas extraction in general, but these mostly haven't received the same level of media attention.

Another environmental concern – not just for unconventional gas but for natural gas more generally – is fugitive methane emissions. Natural gas is mostly methane, and methane is a potent greenhouse gas. There is a risk of methane leakage all through the natural gas value chain, from poorly completed wells to aging pipelines under city streets. If fugitive methane emissions are too large, it could blunt the greenhouse gas emissions advantage of natural gas over coal. (It should be noted that coal mining has methane emissions of its own, as coal seams typically contain methane that is vented or flared before mining.) Significant effort has been devoted recently to assessing the scale of the methane leakage problem and developing sensors and regulations to combat it. Dealing with fugitive methane emissions should be feasible, both technically and economically, but there needs to be the political will to do it.

Opposition on environmental grounds probably won't have a major impact on shale gas activities in the US, which are already well-established. It also isn't likely to be a major limiting factor in China (although high population densities in some potential producing areas could be an issue). However, environmental resistance does have the potential to keep shale gas developments from getting off the ground in other countries, especially in regions that don't have previous experience with oil and gas production.

While shale gas hasn't yet taken off anywhere except in North America, a different form of unconventional gas, coalbed methane (CBM), is an important resource in Australia. CBM (also known as coal seam gas) is gas that comes from coal seams. A well is drilled into a suitable coal seam and the water in the seam is pumped out, which depressurizes the seam and causes gas in the pores of the coal matrix to flow out and into the well. CBM is frequently extracted from coal seams too deep for economic mining of the coal. In cases where a seam is economic for both CBM and coal mining, CBM production can actually facilitate mining by extracting methane that would have to be removed anyway.[25] The US still led the world in CBM production as of 2016, but Australia is predicted to far surpass it by 2025, with some growth expected in China as well.[26]

Natural gas is probably the energy source that could benefit most from a carbon price, because it could help make gas competitive with coal. Of course, a carbon price makes any zero- or low-carbon energy source more competitive relative to coal, but it isn't the most important factor where renewables or nuclear are concerned. Renewables already benefit from significant government incentives even in the absence of a carbon price, and nuclear struggles enough with public acceptance and cost that a carbon price alone won't dramatically boost its prospects.

The impact of a carbon price on coal vs. gas competition has been vividly illustrated in the UK, where a carbon price of £18/tonne of $CO_2$ (approximately $24), in combination with low UK gas prices, helped gas-fired generation displace a massive quantity of coal-fired power.[27] If most of Asia had a credible and significant long-term price of carbon, it could help convince planners and energy developers to choose gas instead of coal. (It would also help a lot if LNG prices remained low or if, even more significantly, shale gas were developed at scale in China and elsewhere.) Without a carbon price, it is hard to see how gas will overcome coal's advantages of cost, ease, and perceived dependability.

Politically, natural gas occupies an uncomfortable middle ground in its competition with coal. Gas is significantly better for the environment than coal, but concerns about fracking, fair or not, have made gas deeply unpopular among some environmentalists. Also, natural gas is still a fossil fuel, and many environmentalists argue that the roughly 50% reduction in greenhouse gas emissions that natural gas provides relative to coal is not enough. Given the need to cut emissions by 80% or more, they argue, natural gas is a dead end, and building new plants that use it locks in emissions that, while lower than coal's, are still too high.

This "good but not good enough" character of gas means it is given little credit for being "green" among environmentalists, while those who don't prioritize environmental considerations at all choose coal over gas for its perceived cost and energy security advantages. As we will discuss in the next section, this can produce a seemingly paradoxical energy development path in which lots of renewables are paired with lots of coal.

## Coal vs. wind and solar

If it were a popularity contest, solar and wind would beat out all other coal alternatives, and coal itself, hands down. Ørsted's "Green Energy Barometer 2017" surveyed citizens of Canada, China, Denmark, France, Germany, Japan, the Netherlands, Poland, South Korea, Sweden, Taiwan, the UK, and the US about their attitudes toward different energy sources.[28] It found that 80% of respondents wanted their countries to use more solar, 67% wanted more offshore wind, and 64% wanted more onshore wind. By contrast, 37% wanted more natural gas, 26% wanted more nuclear, and 14% wanted more coal. In WorldPublicOpinion.org's 2008 survey, which examined a more broad-based sample of countries, a majority of respondents in 20 out of 21 countries (the exception being Russia) said that their respective governments should put more emphasis on "installing solar or wind energy systems" in order to "deal with the problem of energy."[29] Globally, 77% of respondents supported more emphasis on installing wind and solar, whereas only 40% supported more emphasis on "building nuclear energy power plants" and 40% supported more emphasis on "building coal or oil-fired power plants." To most people around the world, nothing says "green" like giant wind turbines in the plains or on ridgetops, or roofs and deserts covered with solar photovoltaics.

The costs of wind and solar have come down significantly in recent decades. Solar photovoltaic module costs have fallen more than a factor of five in the last twenty years, to the point where non-module costs are now the main driver of total installed cost.[30] (Non-module costs include the costs of associated hardware like inverters, customer acquisition, permitting, and installation, among others.) The costs of wind installations dropped sharply in the 1980s and 1990s then showed mixed performance in the 2000s before trending down again in the 2010s.[31] Wind is already cost-competitive with fossil fuel generation in a number of geographies. Some renewables advocates argue based on auction prices for new solar capacity in places like India, Mexico, and the Middle East that solar is already "cheaper than coal."[32] (Understanding exactly what these auction bids signify is complicated; they can sometimes include implicit subsidies to developers, such as access to desirable land or favorable terms on loans,[33] and winning bidders may have made overoptimistic predictions about future declines in equipment prices.)[34] According to this "solar optimist" narrative, solar could displace new coal developments within ten years based purely on more favorable economics.[35]

The fundamental challenge for wind and solar is that they are intermittent – in other words, only available when the wind is blowing or the sun is shining. This implies the need for some combination of backup power (which typically comes from fossil sources) and electricity storage that can capture energy generated during periods of high wind and solar output for later use. How much backup generation and/or storage is required depends on patterns of demand and how much the renewable resources vary over time and space. To take a simple example, if the only renewable energy source in a grid is solar, then none of that renewable capacity can be used to meet demand at night. If wind blows more at night and less during the day, having a mix of wind and solar helps reduce the need for backup generation for solar. Making the grid geographically larger, through transmission lines that interconnect across a wide region, helps too. When sun or wind are not available in one part of the grid, they might be present elsewhere.

However, installing a mix of renewable resources and expanding the grid can only go so far in avoiding the need for backup generation or storage to support intermittent renewables. Even in large electricity markets with a mix of wind and solar, such as California, there are a significant number of time periods with very limited renewable resources. In 2016, for example, there were 168 spells of time where combined wind and solar generation in California was less than 5% of its maximum output.[36] The spells had a mean duration of almost eight hours. Given that electricity storage is limited in California at present, this implies the need for substantial backup power, which costs money. California can import power from the larger western US grid in which it is embedded, which helps a lot, but the state still requires significant in-state backup capacity. (In fact, the challenges of integrating larger and larger quantities of wind and solar generation may drive California to tighten electricity market integration with other western states, which would be a good thing.)

Renewables advocates hope electricity storage will soon be able to manage the problem of renewable intermittency. The idea is that batteries can charge up whenever renewables are plentiful (and electricity prices are low) and discharge when renewables are unavailable (and electricity prices are high). Battery costs have continued to drop, leading to optimism among some observers that the intermittency problem will soon be solved. However, there are two important reasons for caution.

First, battery storage is a very costly way to manage variation in renewable output on scales of months instead of hours or days. In many regions, seasonal variation in wind and solar is substantial. In California, for example, the peak of wind generation in summer is almost a factor of four higher than the low in winter,[37] and solar output is substantially higher in summer as well. Cost-effective storage on these timescales will require development of fundamentally different technology solutions – for example, the generation of synthetic natural gas or hydrogen to use as a long-term energy storage medium. There is still a long way to go to develop long-timescale storage technologies and demonstrate that they can be affordable.

Second, the business model for storage is fundamentally different from that for generation, in that it requires substantial volatility in the electricity price. Generators make money when the average electricity price they receive for generating exceeds their average cost. Storage owners make money when the average price difference between when they charge and when they discharge exceeds their average cost. Electricity market regulators have typically tried to squelch rather than encourage electricity price volatility, and this will have to change for storage to achieve its full potential.

In the absence of plentiful electricity storage on short and long timescales, intermittent renewables face a fundamental problem of value erosion as the share of a certain type of renewable increases. As the share of wind or solar becomes larger, additional renewables of that type provide less and less economic value. When the wind is blowing, all wind units in a certain region will generate electricity. When there is a lot of sun, all the solar units will come on. Where there is no wind, or no solar, none of the units of those types will provide power. Adding more solar units, say, provides no additional value when solar already meets all of daytime demand, nor does it help boost generation at night or on cloudy days, when solar isn't available. Because wind and solar have essentially zero cost of operating (marginal cost), wholesale electricity prices in a competitive market go to zero (or even negative) when renewables are meeting all demand. Even if wind and solar costs decrease over time, they will not be financially viable if electricity prices in the hours when they are generating decrease even faster than their costs go down. This value erosion problem is not too serious at modest renewable shares, but barring major advances in storage, it could have dramatic impacts on the competitiveness of renewable energy at the very high generation shares (50% and above) that California and other jurisdictions have targeted. Coal power plants and other dispatchable resources like gas-fired units do not have this issue because they are available to provide power whenever it is needed (though they are also hurt by low electricity prices, especially coal with its high fixed costs).

As the raw cost of renewable energy continues to drop, intermittency will be the biggest obstacle preventing wind and solar from competing directly with coal. In fact, the "German model," in which countries pair high shares of renewable energy with large amounts of coal capacity, may become more prevalent. Germany has been a poster child for aggressive renewable energy additions, with major growth in wind, solar, and biomass generation. It has also been phasing out nuclear power since the year 2000, driven by the strong anti-nuclear sentiment discussed above. Renewables additions haven't been able to fully compensate for nuclear retirements, so coal generation from both existing and new capacity has filled the gap.

If the goal is reducing carbon emissions at lowest cost – or equivalently, maximizing emissions reductions for the money spent – this approach makes very little sense. Germany has spent a great deal on its renewable energy incentives, but it has thus far achieved no significant reductions in greenhouse gas emissions because the replacement of zero-carbon nuclear with high-carbon coal has canceled out the emissions benefits of the renewables. Germany's renewables efforts may pay global dividends to the extent they drive innovations in renewable energy and management of intermittency, but the renewables plus coal approach is still illogical from an economic and environmental perspective. Phasing out coal-fired power in favor of a less-polluting (and lower fixed cost) option like natural gas would almost certainly provide more "bang for the buck."

There *is* a political logic to the German model, however. Incumbent coal interests are strong in Germany, and coal may still have a significant (if perhaps misguided) "energy security" attraction given Germany's domestic coal resources and reliance on Russia for natural gas. There is also a surprisingly strong political logic to the coal plus renewables strategy more broadly. As shown in the surveys discussed above, most people around the world have accepted the narrative that being green means backing wind and solar. If a government wants to get credit for doing something about climate change, it needs to show it is aggressively pursuing renewables. Germany has attracted more attention for its significant expansion of renewable energy than for its continued heavy reliance on coal. Similarly, India's announcement of aggressive renewable energy plans in the lead-up to the 2015 Paris Climate Conference were largely successful in deflecting international disapproval over the country's simultaneous efforts to expand coal production.

Even as renewables programs receive press attention, coal remains the default way for most emerging economies to build out their power systems. Coal may not be the most popular energy source, but the anti-coal movement in many countries still has a way to go before it catches up to the anti-nuclear movement in fomenting public resistance. Also, coal doesn't have the price or value chain coordination challenges of natural gas. And finally, in coal-producing countries, preserving coal's primary role in the energy supply avoids the need to confront powerful domestic mining interests or make radical changes to the electricity supply industry.

For the above reasons, coal and renewables may in practice end up being politically complementary rather than opposed to each other, even though this combination is far from the least-cost approach to reducing greenhouse gas emissions.

## Coal vs. cleaner coal

If coal is significantly less expensive than competing energy sources, it may be that the cheapest and most practical route to a green future is cleaning up coal rather than replacing it. "Clean coal" means different things to different people. If your biggest concern is local air pollution, clean coal means making sure your coal-fired power plant has technologies like flue gas desulfurization to remove sulfur oxides ($SO_x$), selective catalytic reduction or selective non-catalytic reduction to remove nitrogen oxides ($NO_x$), and electrostatic precipitators or fabric filters to remove particulates. These technologies add upfront and operating costs to coal power plants. However, if the cost difference between coal and alternatives is significant enough, as it frequently is, an efficient coal power plant with good emissions controls may still be more affordable than an alternative energy source.

Increasing power plant efficiency can reduce both local pollutant and greenhouse gas emissions, so highly efficient coal-fired power plants are sometimes included under the rubric of "clean coal." China has made a particularly aggressive push toward higher efficiency coal-fired power plants. Between 2010 and 2016, the majority of the country's capacity additions have been supercritical or ultra-supercritical, with more of the latter than the former.[38] Because of this aggressive introduction of sophisticated modern power plants, the average efficiency of the top 100 best-performing coal plants in China in 2016 was about 30% higher (i.e. 30% more electricity produced per tonne of coal equivalent burned) than that of the top 100 best-performing coal plants in the United States. China's willingness to pay more upfront for efficient coal power plants shows the government's concern with energy security (efficient plants mean less coal is needed) and with finding ways to avoid making a serious air pollution problem worse (efficient plants mean lower emissions, of both local pollutants and $CO_2$).

If the primary concern is climate change, clean coal means capturing most or all of the $CO_2$ from the coal power plant's exhaust and either burying it or binding it up in some material so it is never released to the atmosphere. The technical feasibility of several carbon capture and storage (CCS) technologies has been demonstrated, though their economic viability as a way of scrubbing $CO_2$ from coal plant exhaust has not. The increasingly popular acronym CCUS – for carbon capture, *utilization*, and storage – reflects the fact that the economic prospects of the process are better where the captured $CO_2$ can find a practical use, for example in enhanced oil recovery (EOR) operations. (Injecting $CO_2$ into an oil reservoir can be one way to get more oil to flow to the surface, boosting production.) Environmentalists are generally not enthusiastic about the idea of using captured $CO_2$ to produce more fossil fuels. On the other hand, EOR could serve as a near-term application that would help to drive the development of CCS technology.

*Pre-combustion capture* methods involve converting coal to a gas that can be burned for energy, and capturing the concentrated stream of $CO_2$ that comes out of the gasification process. Capturing a concentrated stream of $CO_2$ is relatively inexpensive, which is the main advantage of pre-combustion capture. (The applications where CCS has already been deployed at scale involve concentrated streams of $CO_2$; the most significant projects are in gas processing applications where $CO_2$ must be separated from natural gas produced from a gas field, as in the case of Norway's Sleipner field.) A major disadvantage of pre-combustion capture is that coal gasification is not an easy process to manage at an industrial scale. The most ambitious attempted demonstration of CCS for coal to date was at Southern Company's Kemper plant in Mississippi. The idea was to use pre-combustion capture of $CO_2$ from an IGCC (integrated coal gasification combined cycle) power plant running on locally produced lignite. The Kemper project turned into a fiasco, and the most significant problems stemmed from the IGCC technology.[39] After a three-year delay and $4 billion cost overrun, Southern Company decided in June 2017 to abandon the plan of using coal with CCS at Kemper and keep running on natural gas instead.[40]

*Post-combustion capture* removes $CO_2$ from the exhaust gases of a conventional power plant burning coal in solid form. The capture can be done with solvents, solid sorbents, or membrane systems. Post-combustion capture doesn't require fundamental modifications to how coal is burned, but it's expensive because the $CO_2$ must be captured from a dilute stream. The Petra Nova facility in Texas, which came online recently, uses post-combustion capture.[41]

*Oxyfuel combustion* is an approach that could in theory reduce cost relative to post-combustion capture by burning coal in pure oxygen and producing flue gas that is 80% to 90% $CO_2$.[42] This method would allow cheaper capture of the $CO_2$, but it also requires cost-effective air separation technology to produce the oxygen.

The Allam cycle is a novel power cycle that uses $CO_2$ as the principal working fluid and would potentially enable inexpensive, integrated $CO_2$ capture. As of 2018, the company NET Power was developing and testing this cycle as a potential low-cost alternative for power generation with CCS, although the first targeted application is to natural gas rather than to coal (which would have to be gasified).[43]

The biggest challenge when it comes to CCS for coal-fired power plants is cost. In 2015, the Global CCS Institute (GCCSI), an organization that produces research on CCS and also advocates for deployment, used data from various sources to estimate the costs of hypothetical power plants with CCS in the United States. GCCSI's 2015 estimates suggested that adding CCS would increase the levelized cost of electricity (LCOE) from a coal plant by 40–100% and from a natural gas plant by 40–60%, but that these higher costs would still be less than those of solar or offshore wind in the United States.[44] Figures from BP's 2018 technology outlook were even more pessimistic about CCS for the near term, suggesting that CCS would push the levelized cost of a coal-fired power plant built today from approximately $30/MWh to over $150/MWh, and that it would increase the cost of a gas-fired power plant from just slightly more than the current coal-fired plant price to over $90/MWh. For plants built in 2050, on the other hand, the BP projections suggest that gas with CCS could be competitive with wind and solar facilities facing high integration costs because of intermittency.[45] (Coal plants with CCS are still not competitive in BP's estimates, a not unfavourable result for BP's business given that the company produces gas and not coal.) Broadly, this is the logic for why CCS advocates argue we will need the technology: it may be expensive today, but it will be among the most cost-effective options when renewable shares get very high and integrating more renewables gets very expensive. CCS also has the advantage that it could help reduce emissions from industrial sectors that may be harder to wean off coal and natural gas. Finally, CCS advocates argue, the costs of CCS are likely to decline significantly as the technology is deployed more widely.

Many engineering-economic models support the basic insight that a low-carbon energy portfolio with CCS may end up being less costly than a low-carbon energy portfolio without CCS. But CCS applied to coal combustion in particular faces a fundamental challenge. The basic attraction of coal is that it is cheap. Adding CCS to coal makes it expensive. It's possible, as GCCSI argues, that coal + CCS may be a cheaper way to cut carbon emissions than some renewable technologies currently being deployed, but this logic fails to account for the different motivations behind coal and renewables deployment. People deploy renewables to be green. People deploy coal because they don't care so much about being green. The combination of coal and CCS does not have a strong political constituency – with the possible exception being the coal industry itself.

The historical experience of CCS development illustrates this basic problem. For a period in the early to mid 2000s, CCS seemed to have broad support in government and climate policy circles as a tool in the climate mitigation portfolio that needed to be developed. The closer CCS came to being a reality, however, the less interested policymakers and the public seemed to be in the expense and risks it would entail. For example, FutureGen was first envisioned in 2003, under the George W. Bush administration, as a $1 billion demonstration project for CCS in the United States.[46] Different jurisdictions jockeyed to be selected, then a site was picked in Illinois, projected costs increased, and enthusiasm cooled off. The Bush administration canceled the project in 2008, the Obama administration restarted it in 2010 as FutureGen 2.0, and then it was killed again in 2015.

Coal-reliant Australia and Germany pursued CCS too – for a while. Australia launched its CCS Flagships Program in 2009, with the idea of funding up to four commercial-scale power plants with CCS as well as some smaller industrial projects.[47] The project award date was originally supposed to be August 2010, then this was pushed back (in large part because of the Asian financial crisis), then the government reduced or deferred funding for the program in the midst of serious infrastructure damage from floods in 2011. Support has been further curtailed since then, and it appears the government is phasing out the program. In Germany, CCS efforts petered out in the face of strong public resistance to storing $CO_2$ underground.

Unless there are significant incentives for CCS deployment, it's hard to imagine that developers will spend huge amounts of money on CCS for coal-fired power anytime soon. When it comes to power generation, natural gas seems to be a more promising near-term target for applying CCS than coal, with cost projections suggesting CCS on gas-fired power plants has a better chance to be competitive with other zero-carbon technologies.[48] If it proves out, the Allam cycle mentioned above could in theory run on gas produced from coal, but it would be easier and more efficient to use natural gas as the fuel.[49] For the moment, at least, the most encouraging developments in CCS appear likely to benefit natural gas more than coal.

## The challenge of replacing coking coal

Coal plays a special role in steelmaking that is not easy to replace. Coking coal (also known as metallurgical coal) is coal with particular properties that enable it to be baked at high temperatures in an airless furnace to form coke – a solid, porous material that is almost pure carbon. Coke is used to turn iron ore mined from the ground into the highly pure "pig iron" that is the key input to steelmaking. The most common method of creating pig iron involves putting iron ore plus coke made from coking coal into a blast furnace (BF), where the coke burns in hot air to form CO, which reacts with the iron ore to remove oxygen from it ("reduce" it), forming ingots of pig iron along with $CO_2$. The pig iron is turned into low-carbon steel in a subsequent process step known as a basic oxygen furnace (BOF).

Worldwide, over 70% of steel is made from primary iron, with the remainder produced by melting scrap steel in electric arc furnaces and then performing additional processing.[50] Of the steel made from primary iron, about 95% is produced using the BF-BOF pathway described above and thus requires coking coal. Considering all the steps from coke production to pig iron production to manufacturing of the finished steel, steelmaking is responsible for about 7% of the total $CO_2$ emissions from human activity.[51] The largest contributor to these emissions is the $CO_2$ produced directly in the reduction reactions in the blast furnace, although significant $CO_2$ emissions are also attributable to the use of fossil fuels – and especially coal – to satisfy the heavy energy requirements of all the process steps in steelmaking.[52]

The carbon footprint of steelmaking could be reduced by generating the energy it requires with natural gas or even non-fossil sources, but replacing the BF-BOF pathway for steel made from primary iron – and thereby replacing coking coal – is not easy. The main existing alternative to the blast furnace, direct reduced iron (DRI), has disadvantages of smaller scale and greater dependence on the quality of inputs.[53] Novel alternatives to the blast furnace are being studied, including reduction with hydrogen instead of coke, but these technologies are at an early stage of development and have not yet proven to be economically competitive.[54] An alternative approach to emissions reduction might be to apply CCS technology to the traditional blast furnace + basic oxygen furnace approach.

## Progress in coal alternatives

There are two important examples in recent decades of large amounts of coal being displaced by natural gas. In both cases, the outcome was produced by the combination of technological change and policies that supported coal replacement. The first case was the UK's "dash to gas" that began in the late 1980s. Between 1990 and 2000, the UK installed large numbers of combined cycle gas turbines (CCGTs), in the process pushing the share of coal down from approximately two-thirds of electricity generation to a mere one-third.[55] This result was made possible by major technological improvements and cost reductions in gas turbines and combined cycle gas turbines between the 1950s and 1980 – innovations that were facilitated by government R&D support.[56] Other factors contributed as well, including the availability of cheap domestic gas from the North Sea, environmental regulations that boosted gas relative to coal, and electricity market restructuring that yielded competitive market players to whom CCGTs were financially attractive.

A second major case of coal displacement by gas was in the United States. Coal's share of total electricity generation fell from 50% to 33% between 2005 and 2015, while the share of natural gas rose from 20% to 33%, with renewables accounting for the remaining portion of coal displacement.[57] This significant substitution of coal by gas was the result mainly of technological innovations in shale gas extraction techniques that pushed down the price of gas in North America and enabled CCGTs to be competitive even with cheap coal.

Both the US and UK examples highlight how cost reductions and policy support are necessary in order for other energy sources to compete with coal. Environmental regulations are certainly important – the UK's environmental rules played a role in helping gas edge out coal – but they only go so far in the absence of alternatives that are reasonably competitive with coal.

Renewables haven't yet had as large an impact as gas in reducing coal generation, but there are a few geographies where they are starting to play an important role. Again, the UK is a notable example. Since the government implemented a carbon price floor in 2013 that ensures a healthy carbon price in the UK even if the EU carbon price is low, coal generation has taken an additional dive,[58] with wind taking up a significant part of the slack.

Aggressive renewable energy targets in Europe and a number of US states, notably California, will result in renewables cutting further into thermal generation, but whether coal or natural gas absorbs the brunt of the reduction depends on the existing fuel mix as well as the structure of environmental policies in place. Without a strong carbon price like there has been in the UK, renewables targets may result in reduced generation from typically more expensive (and lower-emitting) gas rather than cheaper coal.

One reason renewables incentives can reduce thermal generation in Europe and the US and other rich regions is that overall energy demand there is flat or even declining. In developing countries that are trying to rapidly expand their electricity supply, renewable expansions may be able to cut into new thermal capacity additions at the margins, but they may not be able to prevent coal from remaining the fuel of choice, as we have seen, for example, in Southeast Asia. The current situation is a bit different in India because there is generation overcapacity in many parts of the country. To the extent India maintains a power capacity surplus, new renewables can replace generation that would have come from existing coal- or gas-fired power plants. But as long as coal remains cheaper and environmental rules weak, gas-fired capacity is more likely not to run than coal-fired capacity.

Further technological progress will be required before coal is forced to cede its spot as the most important global fuel for electricity generation. For example, better and cheaper options for long-term energy storage would allow renewables to more directly challenge coal. The refinement and spread of techniques for extraction of natural gas from shales could make gas-fired power more economic in Asia. Advanced nuclear reactors and advanced CCS technologies are wild cards that could also play important roles in the future.

## Conclusion

A number of lower-carbon and zero-carbon technologies have the potential to replace coal in the energy supply – and indeed some are already doing so – but all of them have specific challenges beyond cost alone. Hydroelectric and geothermal power, for example, depend on good resources being available in a particular location, and many of the best resources have already been tapped.

Nuclear has serious challenges with public acceptance in most parts of the world, along with massive capital costs – exacerbated by construction and regulatory delays – that make it unattractive for power companies to pursue projects, especially in competitive electricity markets. It is hard to see nuclear challenging coal's dominance until new technologies make these issues more manageable.

Natural gas is currently the second most important energy source for making electricity, and in many ways it is coal's most direct competitor. Gas contributes far less to local pollution than coal, and its carbon dioxide emissions are only about half those of coal. In the United States, where there is plentiful gas from shale, well-developed gas transportation infrastructure, and a market that sets gas prices based on supply and demand, the economics of gas-fired power have become superior to those of coal-fired power.

Because gas transportation infrastructure is so expensive, building a gas value chain requires careful coordination from the gas field to the end user, and investors will develop projects where gas markets guarantee long-term cost recovery. Liquefied natural gas (LNG) is now available in any coastal region with a regasification plant, but the process of converting gas to LNG, shipping it, and regasifying it adds substantial cost for end users. For all of the above reasons, gas has struggled to compete with coal in countries without substantial gas resources of their own.

Wind and solar are zero-carbon energy options with wide public support. Their costs have come down substantially, but in most locations they are not yet cost-competitive with coal in the absence of subsidies. Longer-term, the biggest challenge for wind and solar will be their intermittency – the fact that they only provide energy when wind and sun are available. This means there is a limit to how much wind and solar an energy grid can usefully absorb in the absence of cheaper energy storage than currently exists. This problem will have to be solved through some combination of grid expansion (to average wind and solar output over a wider region), demand-side involvement (so consumers can adjust their electricity use according to real-time energy availability), and improved, cheaper storage. The most significant technological challenge is to develop cost-effective methods of long-term energy storage to accommodate the often-substantial seasonal variations in renewable energy.

Another option would be to keep using coal but capture its harmful emissions so they are not released to the atmosphere. Technologies for eliminating most local pollution from burning coal are readily available, though they are not yet mandated in all countries because of the cost they add. Eliminating carbon dioxide emissions through carbon capture and storage (CCS) is substantially more expensive, and CCS technologies for use with coal have not been proven cost-effective in wide deployment. Still, some energy models suggest that CCS should be an important part of any effort to reduce global greenhouse gas emissions. Even if CCS does end up playing an important role, it may well find wider application to gas than to coal.

As discussed in the next chapter, the strength of policies to support research, development, and deployment will influence the pace of innovation in all of these technologies – and the prospects that alternatives to conventional coal burning will become more broadly competitive in the marketplace.

# CHAPTER SIX

# Policy, Technology, and the Future of Coal

## Why has coal persisted as the "default fuel"?

As I have argued in this book, the primary reason for coal's continued importance, especially in electricity generation, is "BTU arbitrage" – the fact that markets will seek the cheapest available energy source to provide a given energy service. The electrons that power industrial, commercial, and residential energy services are entirely substitutable. Many kinds of power plants pump electrons into the grid, and many kinds of end users draw them out. Consumers connected to large, interconnected electricity grids have no way of knowing where the electrons they are using have come from, and coal continues to be among the cheapest means of providing power at scale in most parts of the world.

Government planners and policymakers have traditionally seen coal as not just cheap and available for the present, but reliably cheap and available into the future – in other words, "energy secure." Many large emerging economies, and notably China and India, have substantial domestic coal resources, and this has given them confidence in the long-term availability and affordability of coal. Domestic availability of energy is probably overrated as a source of energy security, given that most historical energy disruptions have their roots in domestic issues. And as the case of India's coal sector shows, the presence of ample domestic resources doesn't obviate the need for imports if institutional and social obstacles prevent these resources from being fully utilized. Nonetheless, domestic availability has doubtless played into coal's appeal as an energy mainstay in many countries. Even countries that can't rely on domestic coal, like Japan and South Korea, are confident they can always import coal affordably. This is a stark contrast to the case of natural gas, where the historical experience of high and volatile prices on the international market has made countries skittish about leaning on gas too heavily.

Some of the perceived energy security value attached to coal comes from the relative robustness of its value chain. Compared with other fossil fuels, and especially with natural gas, coal's value chain is fairly easy to assemble. Producing gas today requires sophisticated seismic imaging of underground geological formations as well as, often, advanced drilling technology and hydraulic fracturing ("fracking") to get the gas to flow. Modern open-cut coal mines, by contrast, are basically large excavating and earth-moving operations, and more primitive (and often unsafe) mines might involve little more than sending miners down shafts with cutting equipment. Transporting natural gas long distances requires multi-billion-dollar infrastructure – either pipelines or the combination of liquefaction plants, liquefied natural gas (LNG) tankers, and regasification plants at the other end. Coal is transported easily by rail, and in a pinch, trucks will do. As discussed in Chapter 5, natural gas is stored underground in geological formations with special properties, whereas coal can be stockpiled right next to power plants (although coal storage has major issues of its own, including loss of energy content over time and the potential for spontaneous combustion).

The politics of the coal value chain can act to resist any diminution of coal's role. Traditional underground mining is relatively labor intensive, and unions and coal-mining communities try to fight reductions in mining jobs, even when these reductions result from productivity improvements rather than environmental policies. Coal-consuming industries like steelmaking also provide local economic benefits, and these benefits can drive local governments to resist environmental controls that might constrain these industries, as has occurred in China.

The most fundamental tension around coal is between economic benefits and environmental risks. As societies get richer, environmental concerns tend to be prioritized to a greater degree, and this can put increasing pressure on coal. Most rich countries mandate control technologies that reduce local pollution from coal-fired power plants, and emerging economies too are trying to address serious health problems from smog. This is a driving force behind the notional cap on coal use put forward by China's government, as well as its efforts (not always successful) to ban coal heating in areas where it contributes to smog problems in Beijing and other major cities. Concern about pollution is also behind the government's steady development of institutional and technical capability to regulate power plant emissions.

Climate policy could in theory put even more pressure on coal over the long term, given that carbon capture and storage (CCS) is much more expensive than technologies to control local pollutant emissions. Coal plants with controls for $SO_x$, $NO_x$, and particulates can still be cheaper than alternative energy sources, but it is not yet proven that coal plants with CCS can be. As long as CCS remains quite expensive for coal, tighter climate policy is likely to push the energy supply mix in the direction of cleaner alternatives to coal.

## Climate policy and technological change

To date, the political appetite for stringent climate policy around the world has been relatively limited, despite majorities of people being concerned about climate change, at least as expressed on opinion surveys. Around 20% of the world's greenhouse gas emissions are under carbon pricing regimes of some kind, but even within these programs carbon prices remain mostly modest. A number of rich countries have put in place significant mandates for renewable energy, but these policies do not directly address greenhouse gas emissions, and as a result they are not guaranteed to have a strong negative effect on coal use.

For the most part, investors don't seem to believe the world will take strong near-term action on climate change. That's why markets have mostly shrugged off the "unburnable carbon" movement, which aims to convince shareholders that stock prices of fossil fuel companies are inflated by a bubble because policymakers will come to recognize the world can't burn fossil fuels much longer without severe impacts on the world's climate. Skepticism that serious climate policy action will be forthcoming is a major reason why the global power plant pipeline remains so full of coal.

To the extent climate impacts become noticeably more dramatic and visible (though many climate scientists argue they are already dramatic and visible), it is possible that global support for aggressive climate policy would increase, maybe rapidly. But climate change remains a fiendishly difficult problem to tackle, for several main reasons. First, reducing greenhouse gas emissions is expensive (and that goes for non-energy sectors like agriculture as well). When climate impacts are not fully factored into cost, zero-carbon energy is in most cases not yet economically competitive with coal, even for new generation capacity. Replacing all of the coal-fired energy infrastructure that has already been paid for is an even bigger challenge. Second, climate change is a long-term issue, with the worst impacts expected in the future. This makes it more difficult to marshal political support for costly climate mitigation action in the present. Third, climate change presents a knotty collective action problem. If a country takes tough policy action to reduce greenhouse gas emissions but other countries do not follow suit, global greenhouse gas emissions will keep rising, and the country that acts will be stuck with all the costs of acting with none of the benefits of averted climate change. To make matters even more challenging, different countries have different goals, interests, and capabilities where climate change is concerned. Many of the countries that will be hardest hit by climate change are poor and have low per capita greenhouse gas emissions themselves.

Still, the likelihood is that we will see tightening of climate-related environmental policy in the years to come. Different kinds of policies could affect coal in different ways. By directly accounting for the negative externalities of greenhouse gas emissions, carbon pricing could have a significant effect on coal. Under a carbon price, the high $CO_2$ emissions rate of coal would make it less competitive relative to lower-carbon sources. A carbon price would probably help natural gas the most against coal. Although renewables and nuclear are even lower-carbon than gas, renewables have their own strong subsidies and nuclear has its own serious problems of cost and public acceptance.

There are two broad ways to incorporate an emissions price into the cost of using energy: an emissions tax, which directly levies the emissions price on polluters for every tonne they emit, and a cap-and-trade system (also known as an emissions trading system or emissions market), which allocates a fixed number of emissions permits (or "allow-ances") that each allow their holder to release a certain quantity of emissions without penalty. The emissions tax is simpler and more transparent, allowing businesses to more easily plan their investments in emissions-reducing technologies. Cap-and-trade systems have tended to be more politically popular, however, not least because the ultimate cost of compliance is *less* transparent, and there are more potential loopholes. The fact that these programs don't have "tax" in their name is another plus.

Back when the carbon price in Europe was about €30/tonne of $CO_2$, there was appreciable fuel switching from coal to natural gas because gas has roughly half the carbon emissions of coal. More recently, the UK's carbon price floor has helped shift the country's energy mix from coal to gas in a significant way. If global gas prices stay relatively low, a sustained carbon price of $30/tonne or more might be enough to start encouraging countries around the world to build new natural gas generating units instead of coal units.[1]

For all its economic and environmental appeal, carbon pricing has faced significant political resistance. As would be expected, much of this resistance has come from emitting industries themselves, including the coal and power industries. More surprising, perhaps, is that dissension within the environmental community has also hurt the cause of carbon pricing. Environmental economists are near universal in their support of carbon pricing, but other environmentalists have not always been as enthusiastic. Some have preferred to frame the challenges of pollution and climate change in moral rather than economic terms. If emitting pollution or greenhouse gases is inherently immoral, so is buying and selling allowances to cover these emissions; the emissions should just be banned.

Other environmentalists have seemed distrustful of markets and market-based policy instruments because these instruments do not automatically address environmental justice issues – the fact that populations marginalized by class, race, and other factors often bear the brunt of environmental harms. (Despite this concern, there is no inherent reason why the revenue these mechanisms generate could not be used to address such inequities.) Still other environmentalists are simply lukewarm on emissions pricing – not actively opposed, maybe, but more inclined to focus on developing and promoting specific technologies, and especially renewable technologies. This group is convinced the real emissions reductions will come from actively promoting renewable energy rather than relying on technology-neutral price signals to the market.

Washington State's first carbon tax initiative in November 2016 was a dramatic illustration of how environmental groups at cross-purposes can kill carbon pricing. Initiative 732 would have been the first carbon tax in a US state, but it failed to pass after opposition from key environmental groups as well as business interests. This opposition from environmentalists appeared to stem from factors including (1) a resistance to market mechanisms, (2) the "revenue-neutral" design of the tax, which would have reduced state sales taxes instead of generating net revenue, which environmental justice groups might have hoped to help allocate, and (3) the perception that the pro-carbon-tax camp was arrogant in failing to involve environmental justice groups at the outset.[2]

While emissions pricing addresses the negative externalities of energy production, subsidies for energy research and development could help account for *positive externalities* – essentially, the benefits to society from R&D that private parties are unable to fully appropriate. Take basic research as an example. A private company might spend significant money on early stage energy research that could ultimately produce energy technologies with lower emissions and lower costs, benefitting all society. But this company would realize that its competitors would benefit just as much from its research. Therefore, it would decide that it is not in its economic self-interest to pursue such research. Positive externalities like this are a justification for the government to provide support to research and other efforts that have a social benefit but won't be pursued in the absence of additional incentives.

Subsidies for research, development, and deployment can help speed the advancement of alternatives to coal as well as technologies like CCS that could allow coal (and gas) to operate with a lower carbon footprint. Subsidies could be aimed at early stage research that might otherwise go unfunded, or at pilot demonstration projects that are too risky for private players to undertake.

Key technologies that would facilitate shifts in the energy mix away from coal could include those that allow cost-effective management of the intermittency of wind and solar, which will loom increasingly large as renewable shares increase. Cost reductions in batteries could be part of this, though progress in this area is far from easy, and researchers have been working on making better batteries for a long time. Long-term energy storage approaches – for instance, affordable chemical pathways for generating hydrogen or synthetic natural gas to use as an energy storage medium – should also be an important technology development priority.

Currently existing nuclear energy technology is unlikely to displace significant coal in the future. Today's nuclear power plants are too large, too expensive, and too scary, at least in the opinion of a large slice of the world's population.

Small modular reactors (SMRs) are unlikely to compete economically in the short term, given that they sacrifice the economies of scale in generation that have led nuclear reactors to be large. On a longer time frame, though, SMRs could be intriguing. Standardizing reactors and making them "manufacturable" could create significant opportunities to reduce cost. A major portion of the cost of nuclear reactor construction today comes from the costs and delays imposed by a difficult and uncertain regulatory process, which is itself the product of public discomfort around nuclear energy. To the extent that a manufactured SMR might ultimately be perceived as well understood, less site- and design-specific, and perhaps less frightening, the costs of regulatory compliance could come down a lot.

Natural gas could play a bigger role in displacing coal if technologies for extracting shale gas find success outside North America, and especially in China. Until that happens, the cost of shipping gas as LNG will continue to present a barrier to large-scale gas use in much of the world.

Carbon capture and storage (CCS) holds the theoretical promise of letting us continue to tap the world's cheap and plentiful coal supplies without fear of climate impacts. Significant technological progress is needed, however. Today's proven CCS technologies are too expensive to attach to coal, whose biggest attraction is its low cost. Novel CCS approaches are being explored, such as a thermodynamic cycle that burns natural gas and uses $CO_2$ as the working fluid.[3] But even if this innovative approach proves cost-effective, it might find application to natural gas instead of coal.

There has been special enthusiasm for policies that mandate renewable energy. Such policies may boost renewables as alternatives to coal in the long term, but they can have rather ambiguous effects in the short and medium term. Unlike emissions pricing approaches that tax "brown" energy, policies to subsidize "green" energy do nothing to directly discourage the use of dirtier fuels like coal. They also require increasing other taxes to raise revenue to pay for the subsidies. That said, subsidy policies – especially for popular energy sources like renewables – are generally more popular than tax policies, in part because their costs are more hidden than the costs of taxes.

Germany is an example case where a narrow focus on supporting renewable energy coupled with an extreme aversion to nuclear has supported coal's persistence in the energy mix. It seems contradictory to expand cheap and dirty coal *and* expensive and clean renewables, because there is little net emissions benefit, but this "German model" of coal plus renewables has proved surprisingly popular thus far in emerging economies. India seems to be following Germany's lead, as are some countries in Southeast Asia. There is a political logic to this strategy: renewables expansions give a government green credibility, and coal expansions make sure energy is not a constraint on economic growth. Arguably, renewables initiatives can provide international "greenwashing" for countries that wish to continue relying on coal as the core of their power system. By contrast, the middle way of displacing coal with natural gas tends to satisfy neither the "green hawks" nor the "energy security hawks."

Over the long term, the eagerness of rich countries and subnational jurisdictions to serve as testbeds for renewable energy innovation could enhance the ability of renewable technologies to displace coal. The "race to renewables" is likely to result in significant learning when it comes to integration of high shares of wind and solar onto the grid. For example, if California is going to reach its Senate Bill 100 targets of 50% renewable generation by 2026, 60% renewable generation by 2030, and 100% zero-carbon generation by 2045, significant advances will be required in electricity storage and other technologies that support management of intermittency. Batteries will need to get better and cheaper, long-term storage media will need to be developed, and "smart grid" devices will need to be implemented that use energy efficiently – and use it in the periods where energy is most available.

Just as important, market rules will need to be put in place that support these innovations. Energy users will need to be exposed to dynamic prices that incentivize them to reduce demand when wind and sun are not available. These dynamic, volatile prices will also support energy storage technologies, whose business models depend on being able to buy and store energy in low-price periods and discharge it in high-price periods. The hope is that rapid experimentation in rich, enthusiastic jurisdictions – in technology and regulation, on the supply side and on the demand side – will ultimately yield innovations that provide a better range of technology options than those described in Chapter 5. We should expect a less rapid move to renewables in poorer countries, and in many countries we should expect reliance on coal as the backbone of the electricity system for some years to come.

## The future of coal

Some environmentalists are optimistic that we are at or near maximum global coal use already. Global coal use did in fact drop in 2015 and 2016. Does this mean that coal has already reached the point where it is broadly less economically attractive than alternatives? Probably not yet. In countries like China and India where construction of new power plants has at times outpaced demand growth, it can be difficult to tell whether a year-to-year drop in coal generation represents an actual peak in coal use or a temporary drop in the capacity factors of coal plants until demand catches up. For example, China's coal consumption decreased in 2015 and 2016 but then ticked up slightly in 2017 – the result, it appears, of economic and industrial stimulus.[4] A clearer indicator of coal's longer-term trajectory of growth or decline will be whether countries that foresee electricity shortages are still selecting it for new energy developments. For the time being, at least, the pipeline of coal plant construction suggests that they are.

The future of coal will be shaped by the energy planning choices in different categories of countries. First there are the rich, developed countries, where, for the most part, coal use is not going to grow further and will probably decline over time. Germany has still been adding considerable coal-fired power capacity in recent years, but it has signaled that it will not be approving new coal power plants in the future. Like Germany, Australia depends heavily on coal for power generation but does not appear to be planning further expansions. Australia has the luxury of rich and expanding natural gas resources, both onshore, with its significant CBM deposits, and offshore, so it doesn't have particular energy security concerns about leaning on gas. The United States is still one of the largest consumers of coal, and it is likely to see continued declines in coal use on the strength mainly of cheap gas, though renewable additions will play a role as well.

Japan and South Korea are important bellwether cases for developed country coal use. Both are geographically isolated, and both have diversified electricity mixes in which coal plays a significant part. If South Korea and Japan start to turn away from coal, it may be a strong signal that developed country coal use is on its way out, as these countries have more significant energy security concerns than most developed country coal consumers.

China and India are in categories of their own as, respectively, the largest current coal user and the country with the most potential to grow its coal use. When global coal use peaks will depend more than anything else on the trajectories of coal in these two countries. There are signs that China is serious about trying to curtail coal use, including its notional coal use cap, the growing authority and capability of its environmental regulator, its focus on expanding other energy sources, and its seemingly ambitious plan for national carbon pricing. India is starting to lay out plans for more comprehensive air quality monitoring and enforcement, which would certainly affect its coal fleet, though it is much earlier in the process than China. In both countries, the pace of economic growth and the associated need for new electricity capacity may have as much to do with coal's near-term trajectory as anything else.

The fast-growing economies of Southeast Asia and South Asia are the next group of countries to watch when it comes to the future of coal. Whereas the coal growth picture in China and India has been somewhat mixed in the last several years, there is no such ambiguity in Southeast Asia. Coal use there has gone up, and fast. Indonesia and Vietnam have massively expanded their coal-fired capacity, and there has also been growth in the Philippines and Malaysia. In South Asia, Pakistan has been building out coal, and Bangladesh seems to want to follow. Chinese companies and lenders are providing the technology, project management, and finance for many of these efforts.

Beyond these rapidly growing nations is the next wave of less developed countries. These nations too will have to choose where the bulk of their energy will come from.

For the moment, at least, most seem to be choosing coal. Myanmar and Cambodia could represent the next phase of coal-powered development in Southeast Asia. Zimbabwe, Botswana, Malawi, Mozambique, and Nigeria are some of the African nations that have set their sights on expanding coal-fired power.

The challenge for rich countries concerned about climate change is to offer these countries alternatives to coal. Renewables are part of the solution, but they are not the entire solution. No country has yet built out a large, reliable grid based primarily on intermittent renewable resources, and it is unreasonable to expect the poorest countries around the world to be the ones to lead. Until other alternatives are able to provide energy as affordably and reliably as coal – or until rich countries provide financial support to bridge the cost gap to cleaner technologies – the black rock that originally fueled industrial development will continue to do so in many parts of the world.

# Selected Readings

The global energy landscape changes quickly, and this book draws from current reporting in many different periodicals. That said, there are a number of books whose descriptions and analysis are likely to be durable in describing the historical and current role of coal in the global energy system – and which served as an inspiration for this book. For a rich and readable perspective on the entire historical arc of coal, and the problems and prosperity it has always brought, there is no better starting point than Barbara Freese, *Coal: A Human History* (Cambridge, MA: Perseus, 2003). E. A. Wrigley, *Energy and the English Industrial Revolution* (Cambridge, UK: Cambridge University Press, 2010), is rife with insights about coal's early history as a driver of industry development. Vaclav Smil, *Energy and Civilization* (Cambridge, MA: The MIT Press, 2017), traces how transitions from one energy source to another occur, and as such provides invaluable background for thinking about the future of coal (and other energy resources). Richard L. Gordon, *World Coal: Economics, Policies, and Prospects* (Cambridge, UK: Cambridge University Press, 1987), was a seminal examination of the global role of coal as of the mid-1980s. David G. Victor and Richard K. Morse, "Living with coal," *Boston Review*, September/October 2009, crisply lays out the core issue for coal in today's energy landscape, which is the tension between economic development and environmental (and especially climate) goals.

I had the good fortune to co-edit and contribute to a pre-vious book on global coal: Mark C. Thurber and Richard K. Morse, editors, *The Global Coal Market: Supplying the Major Fuel for Emerging Economies* (Cambridge, UK: Cambridge University Press, 2015). Many of the insights in the present book I owe to things I learned from the country and subject matter experts who wrote chapters of that book: Wuyuan Peng, Huaichuan Rui, Gang He, and Kevin Jianjun Tu (on different aspects of China and its coal sector); Jeremy Carl (on India's coal sector); Anton Eberhard (on South Africa's coal sector); Bart Lucarelli (on the coal sectors of Australia and Indonesia as well as advanced coal technologies); Richard K. Morse, Franziska Holz, Clemens Haftendorn, Roman Mendelevitch, and Christian von Hirschhausen (on different aspects of the global coal trade); and Varun Rai (on carbon capture and storage).

In addition to the above resources, Chapter 1 draws on annually updated datasets from BP (BP Statistical Review of World Energy, freely available at https://www. bp.com/en/global/corporate/energy-economics/statistic al-review-of-world-energy.html) and the International Energy Agency (including the data found in the annual editions of *World Energy Outlook*, *Coal Information*, and *Electricity Information*). The energy price data used in this chapter comes from the Bloomberg Terminal provided by Bloomberg L. P. For conceptual background on resource depletion and the nature of energy reserves, see M. A. Adelman (1990), "Mineral depletion, with special refer-ence to petroleum," *Review of Economics and Statistics* 72(1), February 1990.

Chapter 2 draws on various sources about the nature of coal and its role throughout history in providing energy security. For more information on coal formation and characterization, see Heinz H. Damberger, Richard D. Harvey, Rodney R. Ruch, and Josephus Thomas, Jr., "Coal characterization," in B. R. Cooper et al., eds., *The Science and Technology of Coal and Coal Utilization* (New York: Plenum Press, 1994); Stephen Marshak, *Earth: Portrait of a Planet* (New York: W. W. Norton and Company, 2015); and Larry Thomas, *Coal Geology* (Chichester, West Sussex: John Wiley and Sons, 2013). The early uses of coal and its rise as a driver of the Industrial Revolution are treated by Barbara Freese, *Coal: A Human History* (Cambridge, MA: Perseus, 2003), and E. A. Wrigley, *Energy and the English Industrial Revolution* (Cambridge, UK: Cambridge University Press, 2010). Vaclav Smil, *Energy and Civilization* (Cambridge, MA: The MIT Press, 2017), describes the growth in coal's share of world energy over time.

The OECD's energy security rationale for turning to coal for electricity starting in the late 1970s is well expressed by Ulf Lantzke, "Expanding world use of coal," *Foreign Affairs* 58(2), 1979: 351–373. Three chapters in Thurber and Morse, eds., *The Global Coal Market: Supplying the Major Fuel for Emerging Economies* (Cambridge, UK: Cambridge University Press, 2015), describe how Japan's appetite for coal for both steelmaking and electricity played a key role in stimulating the development of coal export industries in South Africa, Australia, and Indonesia, namely: Anton Eberhard, "Market, investment, and policy challenges for South African Coal" (Chapter 5); Bart Lucarelli, "Australia's black coal industry: Past achievements and future challenges" (Chapter 6); and Bart Lucarelli, "Government as creator and destroyer: Indonesia's rapid rise and possible decline as steam coal supplier to Asia" (Chapter 7). China's historical energy calculus for oil is treated by Erica Strecker Downs, *China's Quest for Energy Security* (Santa Monica: RAND, 2000). Wuyuan Peng, "The evolution of China's coal institutions" (Chapter 2 in Thurber and Morse 2015), describes how China's policymakers changed institutions over time in an effort to make sure coal availability didn't constrain the economy. Richard K. Morse, Varun Rai, and Gang He, "The real drivers of carbon capture and storage in China" (Chapter 12 in Thurber and Morse 2015), shows how China's decisionmaking on CCS reflects the desire to avoid negative effects on energy security. Jeremy Carl, "The causes and implications of India's coal production shortfall" (Chapter 4 in Thurber and Morse 2015), and Rohit Chandra, *Advanced State Capitalism in the Indian Coal Industry* (PhD dissertation, Harvard Kennedy School, Harvard University), April 2018, discuss coal-related factors that affect India's energy security. The Coalswarm Coal Plant Tracker (https://endcoal.org/global-coal-plant-tracker/) is a valuable resource for keeping track of the pipeline of coal-fired power plant planning and construction in countries all around the world. To understand why coal use is fading in the US, see Howard Gruenspecht, "The US Coal Sector: Recent and Continuing Challenges," Brookings Institution, 2018; and Joshua Linn and Kristen McCormack, "The roles of energy markets and environmental regulation in reducing coal-fired plant profits and electricity sector emissions," RFF Report, October 2017.

Some of the best discussions of why we won't physically run out of any particular energy resource, including coal, and how the belief that we will can dangerously distort policymaking, come from Morris Adelman and Roger Stern, including: M. A. Adelman (1990), "Mineral depletion, with special reference to petroleum," *Review of Economics and Statistics* 72(1), February 1990; M. A. Adelman, "The real oil problem," *Regulation*, Spring 2004; Roger Stern, "Oil scarcity ideology in US national security policy, 1909–1980," Stanford University Program on Energy and Sustainable

Development Working Paper #105, February 2013; and Roger Stern, *The Lie that Changed History: Peak Oil, Bad Science, and America's Path to the Middle East* (forthcoming). Stern's forthcoming book has an entire chapter on the historical "peak coal" fallacy. Peter A. Shulman, *Coal and Empire: The Birth of Energy Security in Industrial America* (Baltimore: Johns Hopkins University Press, 2015), considers, among other topics, how the presumed need for a network of coaling stations to refuel US steamships was advanced as an argument by some policymakers in the 1800s for why the US needed to colonize other territories. David G. Victor, Amy M. Jaffe, and Mark H. Hayes, eds., *Natural Gas and Geopolitics: From 1970 to 2040* (Cambridge, UK: Cambridge University Press, 2006), includes valuable discussions of energy security considerations around natural gas, which is one of coal's major competitors.

Chapter 3 draws on various resources describing the functioning of different parts of the coal value chain, their health and environmental impacts, and how different steps can interact with each other. Larry Thomas, *Coal Geology* (Chichester, West Sussex: John Wiley and Sons, 2013), and Colin R. Ward, *Coal Geology and Coal Technology* (Melbourne: Blackwell Scientific Publications, 1984), offer good introductions to coal mining and coal mining technology. *Mining Technology*, "The world's worst coal mining disasters," May 16, 2014, describes mining accidents and the factors causing them; and J. Davitt McAteer and Associates, "Upper big branch: The April 5, 2010 explosion: A failure of basic coal mine safety practices," Report to the Governor, Governor's Independent Investigation Panel, May 2011, is a detailed examination of the causes contributing to a particular accident. Peter Burgherr and Stefan Hirschberg, "Comparative risk assessment of severe accidents in the energy sector," *Energy Policy* 74 (2014):

S45–S56, compares historical safety records of different energy technologies.

There are various excellent studies of the social impacts of coal mine development and operation on local communities. A number of such studies for the Indian case are found in Kuntala Lahiri-Dutt, ed., *The Coal Nation: Histories, Ecologies and Politics of Coal in India* (Farnham: Ashgate Publishing, 2014), including: Tony Herbert and Kuntala Lahiri-Dutt, "World bank, coal and indigenous peoples: Lessons from Parej East, Jharkhand" (ch. 7); Kuntala Lahiri-Dutt, Radhika Krishnan, and Nesar Ahmad, "'Captive' coal mining in Jharkhand: Taking land from indigenous communities" (ch. 8); Walter Fernandes and Gita Bharali, "Coal mining in Northeastern India in the age of globalisation" (ch. 9); Patrik Oskarsson, "Marginalising people on marginal commons: The political ecology of coal in Andhra Pradesh" (ch. 10); Prajna Paramita Mishra, "Water worries in a coal mining community: Understanding the problem from the community perspective" (ch. 11); and Nesar Ahmad and Kuntala Lahiri-Dutt, "Gender in coal mining induced displacement and rehabilitation in Jharkhand" (ch. 12). For the Colombian case, an in-depth look at the effect of mine development on a particular Afro-Colombian community is provided (in Spanish) by Liliana Múnera Montes, Margarita Granados Castellanos, Sandra Teherán Sánchez, and Julián Naranjo Vasco, "Bárbaros Hoscos: Historia de Resistencia y Conflicto en la Explotación del Carbón en La Guajira, Colombia," *Opera* 14 (January–June 2014): 47–69. For a review of some of the social and environmental issues of mountaintop mining in the Appalachian region of the United States, see Susan F. Hirsch and E. Franklin Dukes, *Mountaintop Mining in Appalachia: Understanding Stakeholders and Change in Environmental Conflict* (Athens, Ohio: Ohio University Press, 2014).

A number of sources consider coal transportation and its effect on economic and environmental outcomes. Rich snapshots of early coal transport by sea and land, respectively, can be found in Roger Finch, *Coals from Newcastle: The Story of the North East Coast Trade in the Days of Sail* (Lavenham: T. Dalton, 1973), and A. F. Garnett, *Steel Wheels: The Evolution of the Railways and How They Stimulated and Excited Engineers, Architects, Artists, Writers, Musicians, and Travellers* (Waldenbury: Cannwood, 2005). Thurber and Morse, eds., *The Global Coal Market: Supplying the Major Fuel for Emerging Economies* (Cambridge, UK: Cambridge University Press, 2015), includes several studies detailing transportation issues around coal, notably: Bart Lucarelli, "Australia's black coal industry: past achievement and future challenges" (ch. 6, which details historical port development and challenges in Australia); Bart Lucarelli, "Government as creator and destroyer: Indonesia's rapid rise and possible decline as steam coal supplier to Asia" (ch. 7, which goes in depth into Indonesia's water-based transportation economics for both domestic waterways and ocean shipping); and Kevin Jianjun Tu, "A statistical review of coal supply, demand, and transport in China" (Appendix, which provides detailed descriptions of all China's various coal transportation modes). Prospects for new US coal terminals and expanded exports are considered by Sylvie Cornot-Gandolphe, "US coal exports: The long road to Asian markets," Oxford Institute for Energy Studies, Paper CL2, March 2015; and Mark C. Thurber, "US coal to Asia: Examining the role of transportation constraints in energy markets" (ch. 8 in Thurber and Morse 2015). Various studies have considered the effect of railroad regulation on coal market and environmental outcomes in the US, including A. Denny Ellerman and Juan-Pablo Montero, "The declining trend in sulfur dioxide emissions: Implications for allowance prices," *Journal of Environmental Economics and Management* 36 (1998): 26–45; and Shelby Gerking and Stephen F. Hamilton, "What explains the increased utilization of Powder River Basin Coal in electric power generation?" *American Journal of Agricultural Economics* 90(4) (2008): 933–950.

There is a significant literature on air pollution from burning coal and its health effects. Good resources include: IEA, *Energy and Air Pollution: World Energy Outlook Special Report* (Paris: OECD/IEA, 2016); Health Effects Institute, "Special Report 20: Burden of disease attributable to coal-burning and other major sources of air pollution in China," August 2016; Sarath K. Guttikunda and Puja Jawahar, "Atmospheric emissions and pollution from the coal-fired thermal power plants in India," *Atmospheric Environment* 92 (2014): 449–460; Maureen Cropper et al., "The health effects of coal electricity generation in India," RFF Discussion Paper 12–25 (2012); United Nations Environmental Programme, "Global mercury assessment 2013: Sources, emissions, releases, and environmental transport," UNEP Chemicals Branch, Geneva, 2013; Liang Zhang et al., "Mercury emissions from six coal-fired power plants in China," *Fuel Processing Technology* 89 (2008): 1033–1040; and World Health Organization, "WHO global urban ambient air pollution database (update 2016)," available at http://www.who.int/phe/health_topics/outdoorair/databases/cities/en/.

Chapter 4 draws on various sources focused on the drivers and implementation of environmental policy. The following are useful papers from the economics literature on the Environmental Kuznets curve: Charles D. Kolstad, "Interpreting estimated environmental Kuznets curves for greenhouse gases," *Journal of Environment and Development* 15(1), March 2006: 42–29; Gene M. Grossman and

Alan B. Krueger, "Economic growth and the environment," *Quarterly Journal of Economics*, May 1995: 353–377; Thomas M. Selden and Daqing Song, "Environmental quality and development: Is there a Kuznets curve for air pollution emissions?" *Journal of Environmental Economics and Management* 27 (1994): 147–162. The following surveys provide useful insights into public perceptions of environmental problems in countries around the world: WorldPublicOpinion.org, "World publics strongly favor requiring more wind and solar energy, more efficiency, even if it increases costs," Full Report, 2008; Pew Research Center, "Corruption, pollution, inequality are top concerns in China," September 2015; Pew Research Center, "The Modi Bounce," September 2015; Pew Research Center, "Global concern about climate change, broad support for limiting emissions, November 2015; Ørsted / Edelman Intelligence, "Green Energy Barometer 2017." China's deployment of $SO_2$ scrubbers is an important case study of environmental policy action in emerging economies, with the following sources providing valuable insights: Yuan Xu, "Democracy and the environment: A study of China's $SO_2$ emissions goal and $SO_2$ scrubbers in the 11th Five-Year Plan" (PhD dissertation, Princeton University, March 2010); Yuan Xu, Robert H. Williams, and Robert H. Socolow, "China's rapid deployment of $SO_2$ scrubbers," *Energy and Environmental Science*, March 13, 2009; Yuan Xu, "Improvements in the operation of $SO_2$ scrubbers in China's coal power plants," *Environmental Science and Technology* 45 (2011): 380–385. News stories in periodicals provide the most current reporting of how the tension between economic and environmental goals plays out around the world when it comes to coal. An excellent in-depth profile of how a particular environmental group targeted coal in the US is Michael Grunwald, "Inside the war on coal: How Mike Bloomberg, red-state businesses, and a lot of Midwestern lawyers are changing American energy faster than you think," *Politico*, May 26, 2015.

Chapter 5, covering alternatives to coal, taps various resources on different energy technologies (including the public opinion surveys described above). Articles about nuclear power – its historical development and challenges, effective regulatory approaches, and possible technology improvements – include James Cook, "Nuclear follies," *Forbes*, February 11, 1985; John B. Taylor and Frank A. Wolak, "A comparison of government regulation of risk in the financial services and nuclear power industries," in George P. Shultz and Sidney D. Drell, eds., *The Nuclear Enterprise* (Stanford, CA: Hoover Institution Press, 2012), pp. 275–296; Todd Allen, Ryan Fitzpatrick, and John Milko, "The advanced nuclear industry: 2016 update," Third Way, December 12, 2016; Elizabeth Eaves, "Can North America's advanced nuclear reactor companies help save the planet?" *Bulletin of the Atomic Scientists* 73(1), December 22, 2016: 27–37.

For treatment of both the potential and the challenges around further development of natural gas, see: Mark C. Thurber, "Why isn't natural gas in India's climate strategy?" Stanford University NGI Brief, September 2016, https://ngi.stanford.edu/sites/default/files/NGI_Brief_no1_Sep_2016.pdf; Peter Hughes and Daniel Muthmann, "Gas in Asia: From regional premium to global commodity?" Summit Working Paper for the National Bureau of Asian Research Pacific Energy Summit, 2015, http://www.nbr.org/downloads/pdfs/eta/PES_2015_workingpaper_hughes_muthmann.pdf; US Energy Information Administration, "Technically recoverable shale oil and shale gas resources: An assessment of 137 shale formations in 41 countries outside the United States," June 2013;

David G. Victor, Amy M. Jaffe, and Mark H. Hayes, eds., *Natural Gas and Geopolitics: From 1970 to 2040* (Cambridge, UK: Cambridge University Press, 2006); Mark C. Thurber and Joseph Chang, "The policy tightrope in gas-producing countries: Stimulating domestic demand without discouraging supply," Summit Working Paper for the National Bureau of Asian Research Pacific Energy Summit, 2011, http://www.nbr.org/downloads/pdfs/eta/PES_2011_Thurber_Chang.pdf; David Sandalow, Jingchao Wu, Qing Yang, Anders Hove, and Junda Lin, "Meeting China's shale gas goals," Columbia SIPA Center on Global Energy Policy, September 2014.

There are many sources of renewable energy cost data available on the web, for example: the websites of the International Renewable Energy Agency (http://www.irena.org/publications/2018/Jan/Renewable-power-generation-costs-in-2017) and the California Solar Initiative (https://www.californiadgstats.ca.gov/). Some of the future challenges to renewable energy integration are introduced in Alex Trembath and Jesse Jenkins, "A look at wind and solar" (Parts 1 and 2), https://thebreakthrough.org/index.php/voices/energetics/wind-and-solar-how-far-weve-come & https://thebreakthrough.org/index.php/voices/energetics/a-look-at-wind-and-solar-part-2; and Mark C. Thurber, "Gas-fired generation in a high-renewables world," Stanford University Natural Gas Brief, June 2018, https://ngi.stanford.edu/sites/default/files/NGI_Brief_2018-06_R3_Thurber.pdf.

Technologies for carbon capture and storage (CCS) and their costs are reviewed in Global CCS Institute, "The costs of CCS and other low-carbon technologies in the United States – 2015 Update," July 2015; BP Technology Outlook 2018, https://www.bp.com/content/dam/bp/en/corporate/pdf/technology/bp-technology-outlook-2018.pdf; Bart

Lucarelli, "New technologies to the rescue? A review of three game-changing coal technologies and their implications for Australia's black coal industry," in Thurber and Morse, eds., *The Global Coal Market: Supplying the Major Fuel for Emerging Economies* (Cambridge, UK: Cambridge University Press, 2015), pp. 475–556. The new Allam cycle, with its potential in theory for low-cost, integrated $CO_2$ capture, is described in Rodney Allam et al., "Demonstration of the Allam Cycle: An update on the development status of a high efficiency supercritical carbon dioxide power process employing full carbon capture," *Energy Procedia* 114 (2017): 5948–5966.

In addition to the various resources described above, Chapter 6 draws on some specific resources on carbon pricing, including two post-mortems on Washington State's failure to pass carbon tax initiative I-732: Alex Lenferna, "Washington State's carbon tax initiative: Lessons in getting carbon taxes via referendum" (http://www.acad emia.edu/34033360/Washington_States_Carbon_Tax_Ini tiative_Lessons_in_getting_carbon_taxes_via_referendu ms); and Lucas Davis, "Why aren't environmentalists supporting a carbon tax in Washington state?" *The Conversation*, October 30, 2016 (https://theconversation. com/why-arent-environmentalists-supporting-a-carbon-tax-in-washington-state-67740). The World Bank publishes a very helpful annual review on the state of carbon pricing around the world, of which the latest is "State and trends in carbon pricing 2018" (https://openknowledge.worldbank. org/handle/10986/29687).

# Notes

I THE DOUBLE-EDGED SWORD OF COAL

1 IEA, *World Energy Outlook 2017* (Paris: IEA/OECD), p. 648.
2 IEA, *Electricity Information 2017* (Paris: IEA/OECD),
  p II.13–II.16. I defined "developed countries" as countries in
  the Organization for Economic Cooperation and Development
  (OECD) and "appreciable electricity" as at least 1 TWh/year
  (with the vast majority of these countries generating far more
  than that).
3 BP Statistical Review of World Energy 2018, https://www.
  bp.com/en/global/corporate/energy-economics/statistical-
  review-of-world-energy.html.
4 BP Statistical Review of World Energy 2018.
5 BP Statistical Review of World Energy 2018; World Bank Open
  Data, https://data.worldbank.org/indicator/NY.GDP.PCAP.CD.
6 Barbara Freese, *Coal: A Human History* (Cambridge, MA:
  Perseus Publishing, 2003), p. 1.
7 BP Statistical Review of World Energy 2018.
8 Anna Yukhananov and Valerie Volcovici, "World Bank to limit
  financing of coal-fired plants," *Reuters*, July 16, 2013; OECD,
  "Statement from participants to the arrangement on officially
  supported export credits," November 18, 2015, http://www.
  oecd.org/newsroom/statement-from-participants-to-the-
  arrangement-on-officially-supported-export-credits.htm; *The
  Japan Times*, "OECD to end public financing of coal-fired power
  generation," November 18, 2015.

2 THE QUEST FOR ENERGY SECURITY

1 See Heinz H. Damberger, Richard D. Harvey, Rodney R. Ruch, and Josephus Thomas, Jr., "Coal characterization," in B. R. Cooper et al.,eds., *The Science and Technology of Coal and Coal Utilization* (New York: Plenum Press, 1994); Stephen Marshak, *Earth: Portrait of a Planet* (New York: W. W. Norton and Company, 2015); and Larry Thomas, *Coal Geology* (Chichester, West Sussex: John Wiley and Sons, 2013).

2 E. A. Wrigley, *Energy and the English Industrial Revolution* (Cambridge, UK: Cambridge University Press, 2010), p. 37.

3 Barbara Freese, *Coal: A Human History* (Cambridge, MA: Perseus Publishing, 2003).

4 Vaclav Smil, *Energy and Civilization* (Cambridge, MA: The MIT Press, 2017), p. 395.

5 Vaclav Smil, *Energy and Civilization* (Cambridge, MA: The MIT Press, 2017), p. 298.

6 Daniel Yergin, *The Prize: The Epic Quest for Oil, Money, and Power* (New York: Free Press, 1992).

7 US Energy Information Administration, "Competition among fuels for power generation driven by changes in fuel prices," July 13, 2012, https://www.eia.gov/todayinenergy/detail.php?id=7090.

8 IEA, *Electricity Information 2015* (Paris: International Energy Agency, 2015), III-3.

9 IEA, "Principles for IEA Action on Coal," Press Release (79)15, May 22, 1979, http://digitalcollections.library.cmu.edu/awweb/awarchive?type=file&item=583223.

10 Ulf Lantzke, "Expanding world use of coal," *Foreign Affairs* 58(2), 1979: 351–373.

11 IEA, *Electricity Information 2015* (Paris: International Energy Agency, 2015), III-35.

12 Mark C. Thurber and Richard K. Morse, "The Asia-centric coal era," in Mark C. Thurber and Richard K. Morse, eds., *The Global Coal Market: Supplying the Major Fuel for Emerging Economies* (Cambridge, UK: Cambridge University Press, 2015), p. 13.

13 Anton Eberhard, "Market, investment, and policy challenges for South African coal," in Mark C. Thurber and Richard K. Morse, eds., *The Global Coal Market: Supplying the Major Fuel*

*for Emerging Economies* (Cambridge, UK: Cambridge University Press, 2015), p. 171.

14  Bart Lucarelli, "Australia's black coal industry: Past achievements and future challenges," in Mark C. Thurber and Richard K. Morse, eds., *The Global Coal Market: Supplying the Major Fuel for Emerging Economies* (Cambridge, UK: Cambridge University Press, 2015), p. 226.

15  Bart Lucarelli, "Government as creator and destroyer: Indonesia's rapid rise and possible decline as steam coal supplier to Asia," in Mark C. Thurber and Richard K. Morse, eds., *The Global Coal Market: Supplying the Major Fuel for Emerging Economies* (Cambridge, UK: Cambridge University Press, 2015), p. 297.

16  Fred von der Mehden and Steven W. Lewis, "Liquefied natural gas from Indonesia: the Arun project," in David G. Victor, Amy M. Jaffe, and Mark H. Hayes, eds., *Natural Gas and Geopolitics: From 1970 to 2040* (Cambridge, UK: Cambridge University Press, 2006), pp. 91–121.

17  The Federation of Electric Power Companies of Japan, "Historical trend of power generation volume by source in Japan," https://www.fepc.or.jp/english/nuclear/necessary/sw_necessary_02/index.html.

18  Michael Cooper, "Fate of South Korea's new coal plants rests with its new president," S&P Global Platts, May 31, 2017, http://blogs.platts.com/2017/05/31/south-korea-new-coal-plants/.

19  Anna Mikulska and Eryk Kosinski, "Explaining Poland's Coal Paradox," *Forbes*, March 28, 2018; Piotr Naimski, "Naimski: Energy strategy is the sole responsibility of the government," *Biznes Alert*, February 6, 2018, http://biznesalert.pl/naimski-strategia-energetyczna-pakiet-zimowy-nord-stream-2/.

20  Howard Gruenspecht, "The US coal sector: recent and continuing challenges," Brookings Institution, 2018; Joshua Linn and Kristen McCormack, "The roles of energy markets and environmental regulation in reducing coal-fired plant profits and electricity sector emissions," RFF Report, October 2017, http://www.rff.org/files/document/file/RFF%20Rpt-NOx%20Costs.pdf.

21  For a comprehensive review of the evolution of China's coal institutions, see Wuyuan Peng, "The evolution of China's coal institutions," in Mark C. Thurber and Richard K. Morse, eds.,

*The Global Coal Market: Supplying the Major Fuel for Emerging Economies* (Cambridge, UK: Cambridge University Press, 2015), pp. 47–61.

22  Erica Strecker Downs, *China's Quest for Energy Security* (Santa Monica: RAND, 2000).

23  Binbin Jiang, "China National Petroleum Corporation (CNPC): a balancing act between enterprise and government," in David G. Victor, David R. Hults, and Mark Thurber, *Oil and Governance: State-owned Enterprises and the World Energy Supply* (Cambridge, UK: Cambridge University Press, 2012), pp. 386–387.

24  Kevin Jianjun Tu, "Appendix: A statistical review of coal supply, demand, and transport in China," in Mark C. Thurber and Richard K. Morse, eds., *The Global Coal Market: Supplying the Major Fuel for Emerging Economies* (Cambridge, UK: Cambridge University Press, 2015), pp. 624–625.

25  Guy C. K. Leung, Aleh Cherp, Jessica Jewell, and Yi-Ming Wei, "Securitization of energy supply chains in China," *Applied Energy* 123 (2014): 316–326; Binbin Jiang, "China National Petroleum Corporation (CNPC): a balancing act between enterprise and government," in David G. Victor, David R. Hults, and Mark Thurber, *Oil and Governance: State-owned Enterprises and the World Energy Supply* (Cambridge, UK: Cambridge University Press, 2012), pp. 403–405.

26  David Roberts, "The world's largest car market just announced an imminent end to gas and diesel cars," *Vox*, September 13, 2017.

27  Varun Rai, Ngai-Chi Chung, Mark C. Thurber, and David G. Victor, "PESD Carbon Storage Project Database," Stanford University Program on Energy and Sustainable Development Working Paper #76, November 13, 2008, https://pesd.fsi. stanford.edu/publications/carbon_storage_database; Richard K. Morse, Varun Rai, and Gang He, "The real drivers of carbon capture and storage in China," in Mark C. Thurber and Richard K. Morse, eds., *The Global Coal Market: Supplying the Major Fuel for Emerging Economies* (Cambridge, UK: Cambridge University Press, 2015), pp. 557–581.

28  *Bloomberg News*, "China set to displace North America with carbon capture projects," March 28, 2017; Emily Feng, "China looks to capture millions of tonnes of $CO_2$," *Financial Times*, May 21, 2017.

29 *Bloomberg News*, "China set to displace North America with carbon capture projects," March 28, 2017.
30 Richard K. Morse, Varun Rai, and Gang He, "The real drivers of carbon capture and storage in China," in Mark C. Thurber and Richard K. Morse, eds., *The Global Coal Market: Supplying the Major Fuel for Emerging Economies* (Cambridge, UK: Cambridge University Press, 2015), pp. 557–581.
31 Morse, Rai, and He 2015, pp. 568–569.
32 Chinadaily.com, "China to cap coal consumption at 4.1 billion tons by 2020," January 18, 2017, http://www.chinadaily.com.cn/business/2017-01/18/content_27988531.htm.
33 US Energy Information Administration, *International Energy Outlook 2017*, www.eia.gov/ieo.
34 Jeremy Carl, "The causes and implications of India's coal production shortfall," in Mark C. Thurber and Richard K. Morse, eds., *The Global Coal Market: Supplying the Major Fuel for Emerging Economies* (Cambridge, UK: Cambridge University Press, 2015), p. 146.
35 IEA, *Coal Information 2017* (Paris: International Energy Agency, 2017), xiii–xv.
36 PTI, "Coal output to miss govt's target of self sufficiency: Report," *The Indian Express*, October 11, 2016; Michael Safi, "India has enough coal without Adani mine, yet must keep importing, minister says," *Guardian*, June 12, 2017.
37 Christine Shearer, Nicole Ghio, Lauri Myllyvirta, Aiqun Yu, and Ted Nace, "Boom and Bust 2017: Tracking the Global Coal Plant Pipeline," March 2017, https://endcoal.org/wp-content/uploads/2017/03/BoomBust2017-English-Final.pdf.
38 PricewaterhouseCoopers, "Power in Indonesia – Investment and Taxation Guide 2013," April 2013, https://www.pwc.com/id/en/publications/assets/electricity-guide-2013.pdf.
39 Shearer et al., "Boom and Bust 2017," 6.
40 Shearer et al., "Boom and Bust 2017," 6.
41 Ed King, "Vietnam to phase out coal, invest in gas and renewables," *Climate Home*, January 25, 2016, http://www.climatechangenews.com/2016/01/25/vietnam-phase-coal-invest-gas-renewables.
42 Mark Thurber, "The costs of fossil-free development," Stanford University Natural Gas Initiative, Natural Gas Brief #3, https://ngi.stanford.edu/sites/default/files/2017_March_Thurber.pdf.

43  Norimitsu Onishi, "Climate change hits hard in Zambia, an African success story," *The New York Times*, April 12, 2016; *Associated Press*, "Drought-caused blackouts batter Zambia, Zimbabwe economies," October 31, 2015.

44  Coalswarm, The Sierra Club, and Greenpeace, "Boom and Bust" reports 2015–2017, available at http://endcoal.org/wp-content/uploads/2015/05/BoomBustMarch16embargoV8.pdf, http://sierraclub.org/sites/www.sierraclub.org/files/uploads-wysiwig/final%20boom%20and%20bust%202017%20%283-27-16%29.pdf, and http://endcoal.org/wp-content/uploads/2017/03/BoomBust2017-English-Final.pdf.

45  M. A. Adelman, "The real oil problem," *Regulation*, Spring 2004, 16.

46  Roger Stern, "Oil scarcity ideology in US national security policy, 1909–1980," Stanford University Program on Energy and Sustainable Development Working Paper #105, February 2013, https://pesd.fsi.stanford.edu/sites/default/files/WP_105_Stern_Oil_Scarcity_Ideology_08_February_2013.pdf.

47  James E. Akins, "The oil crisis: This time the wolf is here," *Foreign Affairs*, April 1973.

48  M.A. Adelman 2004, 1.

49  Roger Stern, *The Lie that Changed History: Peak Oil, Bad Science, and America's Path to the Middle East* (manuscript draft, 2018).

50  Roger Stern, *The Lie that Changed History: Peak Oil, Bad Science, and America's Path to the Middle East* (manuscript draft, 2018).

51  Bart Lucarelli, "Government as creator and destroyer: Indonesia's rapid rise and possible decline as steam coal supplier to Asia," in Mark C. Thurber and Richard K. Morse, eds., *The Global Coal Market: Supplying the Major Fuel for Emerging Economies* (Cambridge, UK: Cambridge University Press, 2015), pp. 351–352.

52  Franziska Holz, Clemens Haftendorn, Roman Mendelevitch, and Christian von Hirschhausen, "The COALMOD-World model: Coal markets until 2030," in Mark C. Thurber and Richard K. Morse, eds., *The Global Coal Market: Supplying the Major Fuel for Emerging Economies* (Cambridge, UK: Cambridge University Press, 2015), p. 424.

53  James Glanz and Frances Robles, "How storms, missteps and an ailing grid left Puerto Rico in the dark," *The New York Times*,

May 6, 2018; Maria Gallucci, "Rebuilding Puerto Rico's power grid: The inside story," *IEEE Spectrum*, March 12, 2018.

54  Pierre Noël, "EU gas supply security: Unfinished business," Cambridge Working Paper in Economics 1312, April 2013, http://www.econ.cam.ac.uk/dae/repec/cam/pdf/CWPE1312.pdf.

55  Calculations made on an energy basis using data from IEA, *Coal Information 2017* (Paris: IEA, 2017) and IEA, *Natural Gas Information 2017* (Paris: IEA, 2017).

56  World Bank Group, "Carbon pricing watch 2017 (Advance Brief)", http://clgchile.cl/wp-content/uploads/2017/06/Carbon-Pricing-Watch-Advance-Brief-Jun-2017.pdf.

57  David G. Victor, Amy M. Jaffe, and Mark H. Hayes, eds., *Natural Gas and Geopolitics: From 1970 to 2040* (Cambridge, UK: Cambridge University Press, 2006).

## 3  TENSIONS ALONG THE COAL VALUE CHAIN

1  IEA, *Coal Information 2017* (Paris: IEA/OECD), pp. vi–25.

2  BP Statistical Review of World Energy 2018.

3  Larry Thomas, "Chapter 10: Geology and coal mining," in *Coal Geology* (Chichester, West Sussex: John Wiley and Sons, 2013).

4  Barbara Freese, *Coal: A Human History* (Cambridge, MA: Perseus, 2003), p. 21.

5  Colin R. Ward, *Coal Geology and Coal Technology* (Melbourne: Blackwell Scientific Publications, 1984), pp. 17–19.

6  Peter Burgherr and Stefan Hirschberg, "Comparative risk assessment of severe accidents in the energy sector," *Energy Policy* 74 (2014): S45–S56.

7  *Mining Technology*, "The world's worst coal mining disasters," May 16, 2014.

8  J. Davitt McAteer and associates, "Upper Big Branch: The April 5, 2010 explosion: a failure of basic coal mine safety practices," Report to the Governor, Governor's Independent Investigation Panel, May 2011.

9  Mine Safety and Health Administration, "Coal Fatalities for 1900 Through 2016," https://arlweb.msha.gov/stats/centurystats/coalstats.asp.

10  Burgherr and Hirschberg 2014.

11  Yuen Yeuk-laam, "Not breathing easy," *Global Times (China)*, February 16, 2015.

12 James R. Carroll, "Severe black lung returns to 1970s levels," *Courier-Journal (Louisville)*, September 15, 2014.
13 David J. Blackley, Cara N. Halldin, and A. Scott Laney, "Resurgence of a debilitating and entirely preventable respiratory disease among working coal miners," *American Journal of Respiratory and Critical Care Medicine* 190, 6 (September 15, 2014): 708–709.
14 J. Davitt McAteer and associates 2011, 32.
15 Peter Ker, "Coal safety under review amid fears of 'black lung' resurgence," *Canberra Times*, December 2, 2015; Joshua Robertson, "Black lung disease: More cases emerge among Queensland coal workers," *Guardian*, April 6, 2016.
16 Bart Lucarelli, "Australia's black coal industry: Past achievements and future challenges," in Mark C. Thurber and Richard K. Morse, eds., *The Global Coal Market: Supplying the Major Fuel for Emerging Economies* (Cambridge, UK: Cambridge University Press, 2015), pp. 136–137.
17 Rohit Chandra, "Technical and financial evolution of the Indian coal industry (1970–Present)," 2017.
18 United States Department of Labor, Mine Safety, and Health Administration, 2017, https://arlweb.msha.gov/stats/centurystats/coalstats.asp; Christopher Ingraham, "The entire coal industry employs fewer people than Arby's," *Washington Post*, March 31, 2017.
19 Kevin Tu, personal communication, May 20, 2017 and February 8, 2018 (data from China's National Bureau of Statistics).
20 Kevin Yao and Meng Meng, "China expects to lay off 1.8 million workers in coal, steel sectors," *Reuters*, February 29, 2016.
21 Sean O'Leary and Ted Boettner, "The state of working West Virginia 2012," West Virginia Center on Budget and Policy, September 2012, http://www.wvpolicy.org/downloads/SWWV2012_091912.pdf.
22 Jeremy Carl, "The causes and implications of India's coal production shortfall," in Mark C. Thurber and Richard K. Morse, eds., *The Global Coal Market: Supplying the Major Fuel for Emerging Economies* (Cambridge, UK: Cambridge University Press, 2015), pp. 136–137.
23 Jeremy Carl 2015, 126.
24 Rohit Chandra, "Adaptive state capitalism in the Indian coal

industry," PhD dissertation, Harvard Kennedy School, Harvard University, April 2018, 159.

25 Rohit Chandra, "Technical and financial evolution of the Indian coal industry (1970–Present)," presentation at Lawrence Berkeley National Laboratory, Berkeley, CA, September 5, 2017, https://vimeo.com/232896203.

26 Rohit Chandra, "Technical and financial evolution of the Indian coal industry (1970–Present)," 2017.

27 Mine Safety and Health Administration, "Coal fatalities for 1900 through 2016," https://arlweb.msha.gov/stats/centurystats/coalstats.asp.

28 Rohit Chandra, "Renewable energy and its regional consequences," website of University of Pennsylvania Center for the Advanced Study of India, https://casi.sas.upenn.edu/iit/rohchandra.

29 Anna Mikulska and Eryk Kosinski, "Explaining Poland's coal paradox," *Forbes*, March 28, 2018.

30 Dwyer Gunn, "Where should all the coal miners go?" *Pacific Standard*, December 2, 2015.

31 Lauren Smiley, "Can you teach a coal miner to code?" *Wired*, November 18, 2017; Anne Field, "Turning coal miners into coders – and preventing a brain drain," *Forbes*, January 30, 2017.

32 Kevin Yao and Meng Meng, "China expects to lay off 1.8 million workers in coal, steel sectors," *Reuters*, February 29, 2016.

33 Rob Schmitz, "As China's coal mines close, miners are becoming bolder in voicing demands," *NPR*, March 14, 2017.

34 Prajna Paramita Mishra, "Water worries in a coal mining community: Understanding the problem from the community perspective," in Kuntala Lahiri-Dutt, ed., *The Coal Nation: Histories, Ecologies and Politics of Coal in India* (Farnham: Ashgate Publishing, 2014), pp. 219–228.

35 Patrik Oskarsson, "Marginalising people on marginal commons: The political ecology of coal in Andhra Pradesh," in Kuntala Lahiri-Dutt, ed., *The Coal Nation: Histories, Ecologies and Politics of Coal in India* (Farnham: Ashgate Publishing, 2014), pp. 197–218.

36 Walter Fernandes and Gita Bharali, "Coal mining in Northeastern India in the age of globalisation," in Kuntala Lahiri-Dutt, ed., *The Coal Nation: Histories, Ecologies and Politics of Coal in India* (Farnham: Ashgate Publishing, 2014), pp. 183–196.

37  Liliana Múnera Montes, Margarita Granados Castellanos, Sandra Teherán Sánchez, and Julián Naranjo Vasco, "Bárbaros Hoscos: Historia de Resistencia y Conflicto en la Explotación del Carbón en La Guajira, Colombia," *Opera* 14 (January–June 2014): 47–69.

38  Aviva Chomsky, "The dirty story behind local energy," *The Boston Phoenix*, October 1, 2007, available at https://www.organicconsumers.org/news/dirty-story-behind-local-energy; Liliana Múnera Montes, Margarita Granados Castellanos, Sandra Teherán Sánchez, and Julián Naranjo Vasco, "Bárbaros Hoscos: Historia de Resistencia y Conflicto en la Explotación del Carbón en La Guajira, Colombia," *Opera* 14 (January–June 2014): 47–69.

39  Susan F. Hirsch and E. Franklin Dukes, *Mountaintop Mining in Appalachia: Understanding Stakeholders and Change in Environmental Conflict* (Athens, Ohio: Ohio University Press, 2014), pp. 27–52.

40  E. A. Wrigley, *Energy and the English Industrial Revolution* (Cambridge, UK: Cambridge University Press, 2010), p. 103.

41  Bi Fan, "Thoughts on comprehensive solution of coal and power disputes" (*guanyu xitong jiejue meidian maodun de silu*), *Macroeconomic Management* 8 (2009).

42  E. A. Wrigley, *Energy and the English Industrial Revolution* (Cambridge: Cambridge University Press, 2010), pp. 42–43.

43  Roger Finch, *Coals from Newcastle: The Story of the North East Coast Trade in the Days of Sail* (Lavenham: T. Dalton, 1973); A. F. Garnett, *Steel Wheels: The Evolution of the Railways and How They Stimulated and Excited Engineers, Architects, Artists, Writers, Musicians, and Travellers* (Waldenbury: Cannwood, 2005); Donald L. Miller and Richard E. Sharpless, *The Kingdom of Coal: Work, Enterprise, and Ethnic Communities in the Mine Fields* (Philadelphia: University of Pennsylvania Press, 1985).

44  Huaichuan Rui, "Developing large coal-power bases in China," in Thurber and Morse, eds., *The Global Coal Market: Supplying the Major Fuel for Emerging Economies* (Cambridge, UK: Cambridge University Press, 2015), pp. 86–87.

45  A. Denny Ellerman and Juan-Pablo Montero, "The declining trend in sulfur dioxide emissions: Implications for allowance prices," *Journal of Environmental Economics and Management* 36 (1998): 26–45; Shelby Gerking and Stephen F. Hamilton,

"What explains the increased utilization of Powder River Basin Coal in electric power generation?" *American Journal of Agricultural Economics* 90(4) (2008): 933–950.

46  BP Statistical Review of World Energy 2018, https://www.bp.com/en/global/corporate/energy-economics/statistical-review-of-world-energy/downloads.html.

47  Huichuan Rui, Richard K. Morse, and Gang He, "Developing large coal-power bases in China," in Thurber and Morse, eds., *The Global Coal Market: Supplying the Major Fuel for Emerging Economies* (Cambridge: Cambridge University Press, 2015), pp. 113–115.

48  Bart Lucarelli, "Government as creator and destroyer: Indonesia's rapid rise and possible decline as steam coal supplier to Asia," in Thurber and Morse, eds., *The Global Coal Market: Supplying the Major Fuel for Emerging Economies* (Cambridge, UK: Cambridge University Press, 2015), pp. 315–320.

49  Personal communication with Bart Lucarelli, January 28, 2018.

50  Bart Lucarelli, "Australia's black coal industry: Past achievements and future challenges," in Mark C. Thurber and Richard K. Morse, eds., *The Global Coal Market: Supplying the Major Fuel for Emerging Economies* (Cambridge, UK: Cambridge University Press, 2015), p. 251.

51  Sylvie Cornot-Gandolphe, "US coal exports: The long road to Asian markets," Oxford Institute for Energy Studies, Paper CL2, March 2015, https://www.oxfordenergy.org/wpcms/wp-content/uploads/2015/03/CL-21.pdf.

52  Kevin Jianjun Tu, "Appendix: A statistical review of coal supply, demand, and transport," in Thurber and Morse, eds., *The Global Coal Market: Supplying the Major Fuel for Emerging Economies* (Cambridge, UK: Cambridge University Press, 2015), p. 666.

53  *Reuters*, "China coal trucks stuck in 120 km traffic jam," September 1, 2010.

54  Rohit Chandra, "Technical and financial evolution of the Indian coal industry (1970–Present)," 2017.

55  IEA, *Coal Information 2017* (Paris: IEA, 2017), xvii.

56  IEA, *$CO_2$ Emissions from Fuel Combustion 2017* (Paris: IEA/OECD, 2017), xiii.

57  IPCC Working Group 3, technical summary, AR5, p. 42.

58  Other toxic pollutants from coal combustion include lead, arsenic, boron, and selenium.

59 Maureen Cropper et al., "The health effects of coal electricity generation in India (RFF Discussion Paper 12–25)", http://www.rff.org/files/sharepoint/WorkImages/Download/RFF-DP-12-25.pdf.

60 Health Effects Institute, "Special Report 20: Burden of disease attributable to coal-burning and other major sources of air pollution in China," August 2016, https://www.healtheffects.org/publication/burden-disease-attributable-coal-burning-and-other-air-pollution-sources-china.

61 Sarath K. Guttikunda and Puja Jawahar, "Atmospheric emissions and pollution from the coal-fired thermal power plants in India," *Atmospheric Environment* 92 (2014): 449–460.

62 United Nations Environmental Programme, "Global mercury assessment 2013: Sources, emissions, releases, and environmental transport," UNEP Chemicals Branch, Geneva, Switzerland, 2013.

63 Bart Lucarelli, personal communication, January 28, 2018.

64 Edward Wong, "Report Ties Coal Plants to Water Shortage in Northern China," *The New York Times*, March 22, 2016.

65 Liang Zhang, Yuqun Zhuo, Lei Chen, Xuchang Xu, and Changhe Chen, "Mercury emissions from six coal-fired power plants in China," *Fuel Processing Technology* 89 (2008): 1033–1040.

66 Maureen Cropper et al., "The health effects of coal electricity generation in India (RFF Discussion Paper 12–25)", http://www.rff.org/files/sharepoint/WorkImages/Download/RFF-DP-12-25.pdf, pp. 23–24.

67 IEA, *Coal Information 2017* (Paris: IEA, 2017), iv.7.

68 GBD MAPS Working Group, "Burden of disease attributable to coal-burning and other major sources of air pollution in China," Health Effects Institute (Boston, MA), Special Report 20, 2016: 27–34.

69 Wuyuan Peng, "The evolution of China's coal institutions," in Mark C. Thurber and Richard K. Morse, eds., *The Global Coal Market: Supplying the Major Fuel for Emerging Economies* (Cambridge, UK: Cambridge University Press, 2015), pp. 45, 55.

70 Kevin Jianjun Tu, "Appendix: A statistical review of coal supply, demand, and transport in China," in Mark C. Thurber and Richard K. Morse, eds., *The Global Coal Market: Supplying the*

*Major Fuel for Emerging Economies* (Cambridge, UK: Cambridge University Press, 2015), p. 617.

71  Tu 2015, pp. 672–678.

72  Kuntala Lahiri-Dutt, "Between legitimacy and illegality: Informal coal mining at the limits of justice," in Kuntala Lahiri-Dutt, ed., *The Coal Nation: Histories, Ecologies and Politics of Coal in India* (Farnham: Ashgate Publishing, 2014), pp. 39–62.

73  Emily Feng, "China plans fresh crackdown on Tangshan steel production," *Financial Times*, March 27, 2017.

74  Simon Denyer, "Smog and mirrors? China's steel capacity cuts were fake, report says," *Washington Post*, February 13, 2017.

75  Huw Slater, "Coal power and privilege: China's problem with industry-owned generators," *China Dialogue*, May 9, 2017, https://www.chinadialogue.net/article/show/single/en/10040-Coal-power-and-privilege-China-s-problem-with-industry-owned-generators.

76  Josie Le Blond, "Coal resurgence darkens Germans' green image," *Financial Times*, October 12, 2015.

77  Anna Mikulska and Eryk Kosinski, "Explaining Poland's coal paradox," *Forbes*, March 28, 2018.

78  Joshua Linn and Kristen McCormack, "The roles of energy markets and environmental regulation in reducing coal-fired plant profits and electricity sector emissions," RFF Report, October 2017, http://www.rff.org/files/document/file/RFF%20Rpt-NOx%20Costs.pdf.

79  David Roberts, "The US coal industry is going out, not with a whimper, but with a burst of rent-seeking," *Vox*, August 26, 2017.

80  Metin Celebi, Judy Chang, Marc Chupka, Sam Newell, and Ira Shavel, "Evaluation of the DOE's Proposed Grid Resiliency Pricing Rule," October 23, 2017, http://brattle.com/system/publications/pdfs/000/005/530/original/Evaluation_of_the_DOE's_Proposed_Grid_Resiliency_Pricing_Rule.pdf?1509064658; Maximilian Auffhammer and Meredith Fowlie, "Bacon Has Vitamins Too: Why Rick Perry Failed Econ 101 – Again," Energy Institue at Haas, https://energyathaas.wordpress.com/2017/10/09/bacon-has-vitamins-too-why-rick-perry-failed-econ-101-again/.

81  David Stanway, "Mounting debts could derail China plans to cut steel, coal glut," *Reuters*, March 22, 2016.

82  Rohit Chandra, "Technical and financial evolution of the Indian coal industry (1970–Present)," 2017.

83  Louis Preonas, "Market power in coal shipping and implications for US climate policy," Energy Institute at Haas, Working Paper 285, November 2017, https://ei.haas.berkeley.edu/research/papers/WP%20285.pdf; Severin Borenstein, "The cushion in coal markets will make it harder to kill," Energy Institute at Haas, Blog Entry, November 27, 2017, https://energyathaas.wordpress.com/2017/11/27/the-cushion-in-coal-markets-that-will-make-it-harder-to-kill/.

84  Richard K. Morse and Gang He, "The world's greatest coal arbitrage: China's coal import behavior," in Mark C. Thurber and Richard K. Morse, eds., *The Global Coal Market: Supplying the Major Fuel for Emerging Economies* (Cambridge, UK: Cambridge University Press, 2015), pp. 394–410.

85  Huaichuan Rui, Richard K. Morse, and Gang He, "Developing large coal-power bases in China," in Mark C. Thurber and Richard K. Morse, eds., *The Global Coal Market: Supplying the Major Fuel for Emerging Economies* (Cambridge, UK: Cambridge University Press, 2015), pp. 73–122.

86  Jeremy Carl, "The causes and implications of India's coal production shortfall," in Thurber and Morse, eds., *The Global Coal Market: Supplying the Major Fuel for Emerging Economies* (Cambridge, UK: Cambridge University Press, 2015), pp. 130–133.

87  Mani Khurana and Sudeshna Ghosh Banerjee, "Beyond crisis: The financial performance of India's power sector," World Bank Group Report 92490, http://documents.worldbank.org/curated/en/799641468041987190/pdf/924900PUB0978100B0x385375B00PUBLIC0.pdf, p. 35.

88  Carl 2015, pp. 141–145.

89  Rohit Chandra, "Adaptive state capitalism in the Indian coal industry," PhD dissertation, Harvard Kennedy School, Harvard University, April 2018, pp. 73–76.

90  Rui, Morse, and He 2015, pp. 103–105.

91  Peng 2015, p. 48.

92  Shenhua's share of China's production estimated for 2012 using an Arch Coal investor presentation, https://www.sec.gov/Archives/edgar/data/1037676/000110465913022192/a13-7797_1ex99d1.htm, along with data from the BP Statistical Review of World Energy.

93 Peng 2015, p. 48.
94 Huaichuan Rui, "Development, transition, and globalization in China's coal industry," *Development and Change* 2005, 36(4): 691–710.
95 Peng 2015, pp. 58, 66.
96 Anton Eberhard, "Market, investment, and policy challenges for South African coal," in Mark C. Thurber and Richard K. Morse, eds., *The Global Coal Market: Supplying the Major Fuel for Emerging Economies* (Cambridge, UK: Cambridge University Press, 2015), p. 189.
97 Indonesia Investments, "Indonesia consumes more coal due to power plant development," February 24, 2016, https://www.indonesia-investments.com/news/todays-headlines/indonesia-consumes-more-coal-due-to-power-plant-development/item6533?.
98 Bart Lucarelli, "Government as creator and destroyer: Indonesia's rapid rise and possible decline as steam coal supplier to Asia," in Mark C. Thurber and Richard K. Morse, eds., *The Global Coal Market* (Cambridge, UK: Cambridge University Press, 2015), pp. 336–337.
99 Michael Lelyveld, "China crimps energy supplies amid shortages," Radio Free Asia, https://www.rfa.org/english/commentaries/energy_watch/china-crimps-energy-supplies-amid-shortages-06112018102703.html.

## 4 ENVIRONMENTAL POLITICS AND POLICYMAKING

1 United States Environmental Protection Agency, "Greenhouse gas emissions from a typical passenger vehicle," March 2018, https://nepis.epa.gov/Exe/ZyPDF.cgi?Dockey=P100U8YT.pdf – assumes a fuel efficiency of 22 miles per gallon of gasoline and 11,500 miles driven per year.
2 This estimate uses the average 2016 consumption of the average US residential electricity consumer (10,766 kWh, per https://www.eia.gov/tools/faqs/faq.php?id=97&t=3) with the author's calculation of the average emissions rate for electricity generation in the US, computed as the generation-weighted average of the emissions rates in each state (from https://

www.eia.gov/electricity/state/). A more precise estimate would account for the fact that the US is separated into three separate grids, and emissions rates can vary over the year as generation mix and demand vary, but the above calculation is likely to be more than adequate for the present purpose.

3  William D. Nordhaus, "Revisiting the social cost of carbon," *Proceedings of the National Academy of Sciences*, January 31, 2017, https://doi.org/10.1073/pnas.1609244114.

4  US EPA website (snapshot preserved as of January 19, 2017), "The social cost of carbon: Estimating the benefits of reducing greenhouse gas emissions," https://19january2017snapshot. epa.gov/climatechange/social-cost-carbon.html.

5  See https://carbonpricingdashboard.worldbank.org/.

6  Gene M. Grossman and Alan B. Krueger, "Economic growth and the environment," *Quarterly Journal of Economics*, May 1995: 353–377; Thomas M. Selden and Daqing Song, "Environmental quality and development: Is there a Kuznets curve for air pollution emissions?" *Journal of Environmental Economics and Management* 27 (1994): 147–162.

7  Charles D. Kolstad, "Interpreting estimated environmental Kuznets curves for greenhouse gases," *Journal of Environment and Development* 15(1), March 2006: 42–49.

8  Pew Research Center, "Corruption, pollution, inequality are top concerns in China," September 2015, http://www.pewglobal. org/2016/10/05/chinese-public-sees-more-powerful-role-in-world-names-u-s-as-top-threat/10-4-2016-9-39-43-am/.

9  Pew Research Center, "The Modi Bounce," September 2015, http://www.pewglobal.org/2015/09/17/the-modi-bounce/.

10  Pew Research Center, "The Modi Bounce," September 2015, http://www.pewglobal.org/2015/09/17/the-modi-bounce/.

11  Pew Research Center, "Global concern about climate change, broad support for limiting emissions," November 2015, http:// www.pewglobal.org/2015/11/05/global-concern-about-climate-change-broad-support-for-limiting-emissions/.

12  Pew Research Center, "Global concern about climate change, broad support for limiting emissions," November 2015, http:// www.pewglobal.org/2015/11/05/global-concern-about-climate-change-broad-support-for-limiting-emissions/.

13  Bart Lucarelli, "Australia's black coal industry: Past achievements and future challenges," in Mark C. Thurber and

Richard K. Morse, eds., *The Global Coal Market: Supplying the Major Fuel for Emerging Economies* (Cambridge, UK: Cambridge University Press, 2015), pp. 259–266.

14 Pew Research Center, "Global concern about climate change, broad support for limiting emissions," November 2015, http://www.pewglobal.org/2015/11/05/global-concern-about-climate-change-broad-support-for-limiting-emissions/, p. 15.

15 World Health Organization, "WHO global urban ambient air pollution database (update 2016)", http://www.who.int/phe/health_topics/outdoorair/databases/cities/en/.

16 Yuan Xu, "Democracy and the environment: A study of China's $SO_2$ emission goal and $SO_2$ scrubbers in the 11th Five-Year Plan," PhD dissertation, Princeton University, March 2010; Yuan Xu, Robert H. Williams, and Robert H. Socolow, "China's rapid deployment of $SO_2$ scrubbers," *Energy and Environmental Science*, March 13, 2009.

17 Yuan Xu, "Democracy and the environment: A study of China's $SO_2$ emission goal and $SO_2$ scrubbers in the 11th Five-Year Plan," PhD dissertation, Princeton University, March 2010; Yuan Xu, Robert H. Williams, and Robert H. Socolow, "China's rapid deployment of $SO_2$ scrubbers," *Energy and Environmental Science*, March 13, 2009.

18 Yuan Xu, Robert H. Williams, and Robert H. Socolow, "China's rapid deployment of $SO_2$ scrubbers," *Energy and Environmental Science*, March 13, 2009.

19 Yuan Xu, "Improvements in the operation of $SO_2$ scrubbers in China's coal power plants," *Environmental Science and Technology* 45 (2011): 380–385.

20 Kumar Sambhav Shrivastava, "India allows 16 new thermal power plants that violate stricter air pollution standards to come up," *Scroll.in*, October 2, 2017; Aliya Ram, "India admits it will miss coal emissions targets," *Financial Times*, May 2, 2017.

21 Kumar Sambhav Shrivastava, "India allows 16 new thermal power plants that violate stricter air pollution standards to come up," *Scroll.in*, October 2, 2017.

22 Aliya Ram, "India admits it will miss coal emissions targets," *Financial Times*, May 2, 2017.

23 World Bank Data Catalog, "Access to electricity (% of population)," https://data.worldbank.org/indicator/EG.ELC.ACCS.ZS.

24 Kumar Sambhav Shrivastava, "India allows 16 new thermal power plants that violate stricter air pollution standards to come up," *Scroll.in*, October 2, 2017; Aliya Ram, "India admits it will miss coal emissions targets," *Financial Times*, May 2, 2017.

25 As one possibly promising sign, the first conference in India on Continuous Emissions Monitoring Systems took place in 2017 (http://cseindia.org/content/first-ever-conference-continuous-emissions-monitoring-systems-cems-india-help-combat-air).

26 Michael Grunwald, "Inside the war on coal: How Mike Bloomberg, red-state businesses, and a lot of Midwestern lawyers are changing American energy faster than you think," *Politico*, May 26, 2015.

27 Michael Grunwald, "Inside the war on coal: How Mike Bloomberg, red-state businesses, and a lot of Midwestern lawyers are changing American energy faster than you think," *Politico*, May 26, 2015.

28 Jessica Yarnall Loarie and Kelly Change, "BNSF derailed: Train company must finally pay the price for dumping coal into Washington's waterways," Sierra Club website, April 3, 2017, http://www.sierraclub.org/planet/2017/04/bnsf-derailed-train-company-must-finally-pay-price-for-dumping-coal-washington-s.

29 Notably, if one assumes that Asian demand for coal is inelastic over the short and long term because there are few alternatives to coal, it is conceivable that building Pacific Northwest ports could even *decrease* global coal use by driving up coal prices in North America and Europe, where natural gas is a more readily available alternative to coal – see Frank A. Wolak, "Modeling the world coal market," draft paper November 2017.

30 Deborah Doan, "The Indian government has shut the door on NGOs," *Guardian*, September 7, 2016.

31 David Stanway and Sue-Lin Wong, "Smoke and mirrors: Beijing battles to control smog message," *Reuters*, February 15, 2017.

32 https://endcoal.org/global-coal-plant-tracker/.

33 Christophe McGlade and Paul Ekins, "The geographical distribution of fossil fuels unused when limiting global warming to 2°C," *Nature* 517 (2015): 187–190.

34 Stanford News, "Stanford to divest from coal companies," Stanford Report, May 6, 2014, http://news.stanford.edu/news/2014/may/divest-coal-trustees-050714.html.

35 Stanford News, "Stanford and climate change: A statement of

the Board of Trustees," April 25, 2016, http://news.stanford.edu/2016/04/25/stanford-climate-change-statement-board-trustees/.

36  Adam Ashton, "California pension fund divests from coal as industry rebounds," *The Sacramento Bee*, August 7, 2017.

37  Damian Carrington, "Norway confirms $900bn sovereign wealth fund's major coal divestment," *Guardian*, June 5, 2015.

38  Attracta Mooney, "Growing number of pension funds divest from fossil fuels," *Financial Times*, April 27, 2017.

39  *Agence France-Presse*, "World's biggest wealth fund excludes 52 coal-related groups," April 15, 2016.

40  Paul Hockenos, "Germany's dirty secret: Climate activists take aim at Europe's largest coal industry," *The Nation*, August 29, 2017.

41  OECD, "Statement from participants to the arrangement on officially supported export credits," November 18, 2015, http://www.oecd.org/newsroom/statement-from-participants-to-the-arrangement-on-officially-supported-export-credits.htm; *The Japan Times*, "OECD to end public financing of coal-fired power generation," November 18, 2015.

42  Anna Yukhananov and Valerie Volcovici, "World Bank to limit financing of coal-fired plants," *Reuters*, July 16, 2013.

43  Zack Colman, "Trump admin to launch 'clean coal' effort," *E&E News*, December 11, 2017.

44  Jean Chemnick, "Bank expected to exit coal with 'zombie' Kosovo project," *E&E News*, June 14, 2018.

45  Michael Slezak, "Asia's coal-fired power boom 'bankrolled by foreign governments and banks,'" *Guardian*, July 20, 2017.

46  Han Chen, "Why are G20 governments financing coal over renewables?" NRDC Expert Blog, July 17, 2017, https://www.nrdc.org/experts/han-chen/why-are-g20-governments-financing-coal-over-renewables.

47  Nithin Coca, "Asia and the fall of coal," *The Diplomat*, June 22, 2017.

48  Hiroko Tabuchi, "As Beijing joins climate fight, Chinese companies build coal plants," *The New York Times*, July 1, 2017.

49  Anton Eberhard, "Market, investment, and policy challenges for South African coal," in Mark C. Thurber and Richard K. Morse, eds., *The Global Coal Market: Supplying the Major Fuel*

*for Emerging Economies* (Cambridge, UK: Cambridge University Press, 2015), pp. 177–178.

50 Siseko Njobeni, "Hogan confident of UK vote for Eskom plant load," *Business Day (South Africa)*, May 15, 2010.

51 *Mail and Guardian*, "Medupi: Hogan answers questions on World Bank loan," May 11, 2010.

52 Lisa Friedman, "World Bank: US to abstain on South African Coal Plant," *Climate Wire*, April 8, 2010.

53 Kamini Padayachee, "Eskom loan 'will foul the air,'" *The Mercury (South Africa)*, December 15, 2009.

54 Celia W. Dugger, "Energy needs in South Africa collide with Obama policy," *The New York Times*, April 7, 2010.

55 Lisa Friedman, "South Africa wins $3.75 billion coal loan," *The New York Times*, April 9, 2010.

56 Lisa Friedman, "US to abstain on South African coal plant," *Climate Wire*, April 8, 2010.

### 5 ALTERNATIVES TO COAL

1 IEA, *World Energy Outlook 2017*, p. 672.

2 Peter Burgherr and Stefan Hirschberg, "Comparative risk assessment of severe accidents in the energy sector," *Energy Policy* 74 (2014): S45–S56; Clean Air Task Force, "The toll from coal," September 2010, http://www.catf.us/resources/publications/files/The_Toll_from_Coal.pdf.

3 WorldPublicOpinion.org, "World publics strongly favor requiring more wind and solar energy, more efficiency, even if it increases costs," Full Report, 2008, http://worldpublicopinion.net/wp-content/uploads/2016/04/WPO_Energy_Nov08_longart.pdf.

4 *The Economist*, "Nuclear activism: Limiting the fallout," July 20, 2013; Brian Hioe, "Anti-Nuclear Protests in China?" *New Bloom*, August 14, 2016.

5 Se Young Jang, "South Korea's nuclear energy debate," *The Diplomat*, October 26, 2017.

6 Ørsted / Edelman Intelligence, "Green Energy Barometer 2017," https://orsted.com/-/media/WWW/Docs/Corp/COM/Barometer-campaign/Green-Energy-Barometer-2017_with-appendix.ashx?la=en&hash=65C5D0F30494C277249CA7622AF0229AD5B6D3CB.

7 John B. Taylor and Frank A. Wolak, "A comparison of government regulation of risk in the financial services and nuclear power industries," in George P. Shultz and Sidney D. Drell, eds., *The Nuclear Enterprise* (Stanford, CA: Hoover Institution Press, 2012), pp. 275–296.

8 James Cook, "Nuclear Follies," *Forbes*, February 11, 1985.

9 Steven Mufson, "Georgia regulatory staff calls the last US nuclear construction project uneconomic," *The Washington Post*, December 5, 2017.

10 Andrew Ward, "Nuclear plant nears completion after huge delays," *Financial Times*, May 17, 2017.

11 Kiran Stacey, "EDF Faces State Aid Hurdle over Hinkley Point Project," *Financial Times*, April 22, 2016; Michael Stothard, "Nuclear reactor clean-up weighs on EDF," *Financial Times*, April 19, 2016; Andrew Ward, "Nuclear plant nears completion after huge delays," *Financial Times*, May 17, 2017.

12 Andrew Ward, "Nuclear plant nears completion after huge delays," *Financial Times*, May 17, 2017.

13 Samuel Brinton, "The advanced nuclear industry," Third Way, June 15, 2015, http://www.thirdway.org/report/the-advanced-nuclear-industry; Todd Allen, Ryan Fitzpatrick, and John Milko, "The advanced nuclear industry: 2016 Update," Third Way, December 12, 2016, http://www.thirdway.org/infographic/the-advanced-nuclear-industry-2016-update.

14 Elizabeth Eaves, "Can North America's advanced nuclear reactor companies help save the planet?" *Bulletin of the Atomic Scientists* 73(1), December 22, 2016: 27–37.

15 IGU, "2017 World LNG Report," https://www.igu.org/sites/default/files/103419-World_IGU_Report_no%20crops.pdf.

16 Fritz Crotogino, "Traditional bulk energy storage – coal and underground natural gas and oil storage," in Trevor M. Letcher, ed., *Storing Energy* (Elsevier, 2016), pp. 391–409.

17 Brad Plumer, "Trump orders a lifeline for struggling coal and nuclear plants," *The New York Times*, June 1, 2018.

18 Mark C. Thurber and Joseph Chang, "The policy tightrope in gas-producing countries: stimulating domestic demand without discouraging supply," Summit Working Paper for the National Bureau of Asian Research Pacific Energy Summit, 2011, http://www.nbr.org/downloads/pdfs/eta/PES_2011_Thurber_Chang.pdf.

19  See, for example, Peter Hughes and Daniel Muthmann, "Gas in Asia: From regional premium to global commodity?" Summit Working Paper for the National Bureau of Asian Research Pacific Energy Summit, 2015, http://nbr.org/downloads/pdfs/eta/PES_2015_workingpaper_hughes_muthmann.pdf.

20  Thurber and Chang 2011.

21  Mark Thurber, "Why isn't natural gas in India's climate strategy?" Stanford University Natural Gas Initiative, Natural Gas Brief #1, 2016, https://ngi.stanford.edu/sites/default/files/NGI_Brief_no1_Sep_2016.pdf.

22  US Energy Information Administration, "Technically recoverable shale oil and shale gas resources: An assessment of 137 shale formations in 41 countries outside the United States," June 2013, https://www.eia.gov/analysis/studies/worldshalegas/archive/2013/pdf/fullreport_2013.pdf.

23  David Sandalow, Jingchao Wu, Qing Yang, Anders Hove, and Junda Lin, "Meeting China's shale gas goals," Columbia SIPA Center on Global Energy Policy, September 2014, http://energypolicy.columbia.edu/sites/default/files/China%20Shale%20Gas_WORKING%20DRAFT_Sept%2011.pdf.

24  Ben Geman, "Gas drilling is polluting water, but don't blame fracking," The Atlantic, September 15, 2014, https://www.theatlantic.com/politics/archive/2014/09/gas-drilling-is-polluting-water-but-dont-blame-fracking/446961/.

25  Bart Lucarelli, "New technologies to the rescue? A review of three game-changing coal technologies and their implications for Australia's black coal industry," in Mark C. Thurber and Richard K. Morse, eds., The Global Coal Market: Supplying the Major Fuel for Emerging Economies (Cambridge, UK: Cambridge University Press, 2015), pp. 538–539.

26  IEA, World Energy Outlook 2017 (Paris: IEA, 2017), 349.

27  Simon Evans, "Factcheck: The carbon floor price and household energy bills," Carbon Brief, September 29, 2016, https://www.carbonbrief.org/factcheck-carbon-floor-price-household-energy-bills; Simon Evans, "'Huge' coal-to-gas switch drives down EU power emissions," Carbon Brief, January 25, 2017, https://www.carbonbrief.org/huge-coal-gas-switch-drives-down-eu-emissions.

28  Ørsted / Edelman Intelligence, "Green Energy Barometer 2017," https://orsted.com/-/media/WWW/Docs/Corp/COM/

Barometer-campaign/Green-Energy-Barometer-2017_with-appendix.ashx?la=en&hash=65C5D0F30494C277249CA7622A F0229AD5B6D3CB.

29  WorldPublicOpinion.org, "World publics strongly favor requiring more wind and solar energy, more efficiency, even if it increases costs," Full Report, 2008, http://worldpublicopinion. net/wp-content/uploads/2016/04/WPO_Energy_Nov08_longart.pdf.

30  Galen Barose and Naïm Darghouth, "Tracking the Sun IX: The installed price of residential and non-residential photovoltaic systems in the United States," August 2016.

31  Ryan Wiser, Karen Jenni, Joachim Seel, Erin Baker, Maureen Hand, Eric Lantz, and Aaron Smith, "Forecasting wind energy costs and cost drivers: The views of the world's leading experts," Report LNBL-1005717, June 2016: 34–36.

32  The use of winning auction bid prices as proxies for levelized cost of energy (LCOE) can be problematic for a number of reasons, including the fact that these bids could factor in hidden subsidies and also that the ultimate profitability of the projects at the bid prices may not be known until later.

33  Rohit Chandra, "Technical and financial evolution of the Indian coal industry (1970–Present)," 2017.

34  Jason Deign, "India's record-low wind and solar prices may not be sustainable," *Greentech Media*, September 25, 2017.

35  See, for example, Jess Shankleman and Chris Martin, "Solar could beat coal to become the cheapest power on earth," *Bloomberg*, January 3, 2017.

36  Data from California ISO.

37  US Energy Information Administration, "Wind generation seasonal patterns vary across the United States," February 25, 2015, https://www.eia.gov/todayinenergy/detail.php?id=20112.

38  Melanie Hart, Luke Bassett, and Blaine Johnson, "Everything you think you know about coal in China is wrong," Center for American Progress, May 15, 2017, https://www.americanprogress.org/issues/green/reports/2017/05/15/432141/everything-think-know-coal-china-wrong/.

39  Laszlo Varro, "Commentary: We can't let Kemper slow the progress of carbon capture," IEA website, July 7, 2017, https://www.iea.org/newsroom/news/2017/july/

commentary-we-cant-let-kemper-slow-the-progress-of-carbon-capture-and-storage.html.

40  Katie Fehrenbacher, "Carbon capture suffers a huge setback as Kemper plant suspends work," *Greentech Media*, June 29, 2017, https://www.greentechmedia.com/articles/read/carbon-capture-suffers-a-huge-setback-as-kemper-plant-suspends-work#gs.qF_WhLw.

41  Katie Fehrenbacher, "Carbon capture suffers a huge setback as Kemper plant suspends work," 2017.

42  Bart Lucarelli, "New technologies to the rescue? A review of three game-changing coal technologies and their implications for Australia's black coal industry," in Mark C. Thurber and Richard K. Morse, eds., *The Global Coal Market: Supplying the Major Fuel for Emerging Economies* (Cambridge, UK: Cambridge University Press, 2015), p. 519.

43  At the time of writing, NET Power was testing a demonstration plant in Texas.

44  Global CCS Institute, "The Costs of CCS and Other Low-Carbon Technologies in the United States – 2015 Update," July 2015, http://hub.globalccsinstitute.com/sites/default/files/publications/195008/costs-ccs-other-low-carbon-technologies-united-states-2015-update.pdf, pp. 9–10.

45  BP Technology Outlook 2018, https://www.bp.com/content/dam/bp/en/corporate/pdf/technology/bp-technology-outlook-2018.pdf, p. 34.

46  Ari Natter, "DOE suspends $1 billion in FutureGen funds, killing carbon capture demonstration project," *Bloomberg BNA*, February 5, 2015.

47  Bart Lucarelli, "New technologies to the rescue? A review of three game-changing coal technologies and their implications for Australia's black coal industry," 2015: 523–524.

48  BP Technology Outlook 2018, https://www.bp.com/content/dam/bp/en/corporate/pdf/technology/bp-technology-outlook-2018.pdf, p. 34.

49  The coal would have to be gasified, reducing efficiency and increasing costs.

50  World Steel Association, "World steel in figures 2017," 2017.

51  Yeonbae Kim and Ernst Worrell, "International comparison of $CO_2$ emission trends in the iron and steel industry," *Energy Policy* 30 (2002): 827–838.

52 Andreas Orth, Nikola Anastasijevic, and Heinz Eichberger, "Low $CO_2$ emission technologies for iron and steelmaking as well as titania slag production," *Minerals Engineering* 20 (2007): 854–861.

53 Hong Yong Sohn and Yousef Mohassab, "Greenhouse gas emissions and energy consumption of ironmaking processes," in P. Cavaliere, ed., *Ironmaking and Steelmaking Processes* (Switzerland: Springer, 2016), pp. 427–455.

54 Intergovernmental Panel on Climate Change Working Group III, "IPCC Fourth Assessment Report: Climate Change 2007 – Section 7.4.1 Iron and Steel," 2007.

55 Florian Kern, "The development of the CCGT and the 'dash to gas' in the UK power industry (1987–2000)," UK Energy Research Centre report UKERC/RS/CCS/2012/2009, February 2012, http://citeseerx.ist.psu.edu/viewdoc/download?doi=10.1.1.645.1366&rep=rep1&type=pdf.

56 Arnulf Grübler, Nebojša Nakićenović, and David G. Victor, "Dynamics of energy technologies and global change," *Energy Policy* 27 (1999): 247–280.

57 US Energy Information Administration, "Natural gas expected to surpass coal in mix of fuel used for US power generation in 2016," March 16, 2016, https://www.eia.gov/todayinenergy/detail.php?id=25392.

58 David Hirst, "Carbon Price Floor (CPF) and the pricing support mechanism," House of Commons Library Briefing Paper Number 05927, researchbriefings.files.parliament.uk/documents/SN05927/SN05927.pdf.

6 POLICY, TECHNOLOGY, AND THE FUTURE OF COAL

1 Mark Thurber, "Why isn't natural gas in India's climate strategy?" Stanford University Natural Gas Initiative Natural Gas Brief #1, September 2016, https://ngi.stanford.edu/briefs.

2 Alex Lenferna, "Washington State's Carbon Tax Initiative: Lessons in getting carbon taxes via referendums," *Public Administration Review*, 2017, https://publicadministrationreview.org/climate-change-symposium-washington-state-carbon-tax/; Lucas Davis, "Why aren't environmentalists

supporting a carbon tax in Washington state?" The Berkeley Blog, October 31, 2016, http://blogs.berkeley.edu/2016/10/31/why-arent-environmentalists-supporting-a-carbon-tax-in-washington-state/.

3  This is the "Allam cycle" pioneered by NET Power.
4  Feng Hao, Lili Pike, and Yao Zhe, "China's coal consumption grows slightly," *China Dialogue*, February 28, 2018.

# Index